POETRY FROM CRESCENT MOON

William Shakespeare: *The Sonnets*
edited, with an introduction by Mark Tuley

William Shakespeare: *Complete Poems*
edited and introduced by Mark Tuley

Shakespeare: Love, Poetry and Magic in Shakespeare's Sonnets and Plays
by B.D. Barnacle

Elizabethan Sonnet Cycles
edited and introduced by Mark Tuley

Edmund Spenser: *Heavenly Love: Selected Poems*
selected and introduced by Teresa Page

Edmund Spenser: *Amoretti*
edited by Teresa Page

Robert Herrick: *Delight In Disorder: Selected Poems*
edited and introduced by M.K. Pace

Sir Thomas Wyatt: *Love For Love: Selected Poems*
selected and introduced by Louise Cooper

John Donne: *Air and Angels: Selected Poems*
selected and introduced by A.H. Ninham

D.H. Lawrence: *Being Alive: Selected Poems*
edited with an introduction by Margaret Elvy

D.H. Lawrence: Symbolic Landscapes
by Jane Foster

D.H. Lawrence: Infinite Sensual Violence
by M.K. Pace

Percy Bysshe Shelley: *Paradise of Golden Lights: Selected Poems*
selected and introduced by Charlotte Greene

Thomas Hardy: *Her Haunting Ground: Selected Poems*
edited, with an introduction by A.H. Ninham

Sexing Hardy: Thomas Hardy and Feminism
by Margaret Elvy

Emily Bronte: *Darkness and Glory: Selected Poems*
selected and introduced by Miriam Chalk

John Keats: *Bright Star: Selected Poems*
edited with an introduction by Miriam Chalk

John Keats: *Poems of 1820*
edited with an introduction by Miriam Chalk

Henry Vaughan: *A Great Ring of Pure and Endless Light: Selected Poems*
selected and introduced by A.H. Ninham

The Crescent Moon Book of Love Poetry
edited by Louise Cooper

The Crescent Moon Book of Mystical Poetry in English
edited by Carol Appleby

The Crescent Moon Book of Nature Poetry From Langland to Lawrence
edited by Margaret Elvy

The Crescent Moon Book of Metaphysical Poetry
edited and introduced by Charlotte Greene

The Crescent Moon Book of Elizabethan Love Poetry
edited and introduced by Carol Appleby

The Crescent Moon Book of Romantic Poetry
edited and introduced by L.M. Poole

Peter Redgrove: Here Comes the Flood
by Jeremy Mark Robinson

Sex-Magic-Poetry-Cornwall: A Flood of Poems
by Peter Redgrove, edited with an essay by Jeremy Mark Robinson

Brigitte's Blue Heart
by Jeremy Reed

Claudia Schiffer's Red Shoes
by Jeremy Reed

By-Blows: Uncollected Poems
by D.J. Enright

Petrarch, Dante and the Troubadours: The Religion of Love and Poetry
by Cassidy Hughes

Dante: *Selections From the Vita Nuova*
translated by Thomas Okey

Arthur Rimbaud: *Selected Poems*
edited and translated by Andrew Jary

Arthur Rimbaud: *A Season in Hell*
edited and translated by Andrew Jary

Rimbaud: Arthur Rimbaud and the Magic of Poetry
by Jeremy Mark Robinson

Friedrich Hölderlin: *Hölderlin's Songs of Light: Selected Poems*
translated by Michael Hamburger

Rainer Maria Rilke: *Dance the Orange:* Selected Poems
translated by Michael Hamburger

Rilke: Space, Essence and Angels in the Poetry of Rainer Maria Rilke
by B.D. Barnacle

German Romantic Poetry: Goethe, Novalis, Heine, Hölderlin
by Carol Appleby

Arseny Tarkovsky: *Life, Life: Selected Poems*
translated by Virginia Rounding

Emily Dickinson: *Wild Nights: Selected Poems*
selected and introduced by Miriam Chalk

Cavafy: Anatomy of a Soul
by Matt Crispin

Elizabethan Sonnet Cycles Two

ELIZABETHAN SONNET CYCLES

VOLUME TWO

Henry Constable
Giles Fletcher
Bartholomew Griffin
Thomas Lodge
William Smith

Edited by Mark Tuley
Introduced by Martha Foote Crow

CRESCENT MOON

CRESCENT MOON PUBLISHING
P.O. Box 1312, Maidstone
Kent, ME14 5XU
Great Britain
ww.crmoon.com

First published 2017.

Printed and bound in the U.S.A.
Set in Bodoni Book 11 on 13pt.
Designed by Radiance Graphics.

British Library Cataloguing in Publication data

ISBN-13 9781861715791 (Pbk)
ISBN-13 9781861716965 (Hbk)

CONTENTS

A NOTE ON THE TEXT

The text comes from *Elizabethan Sonnet-Cycles*, edited by Martha Foote Crow, published by Kegan Paul, Trench, Trübner & Co., London, 1896/97.

Two views of London around 1600.

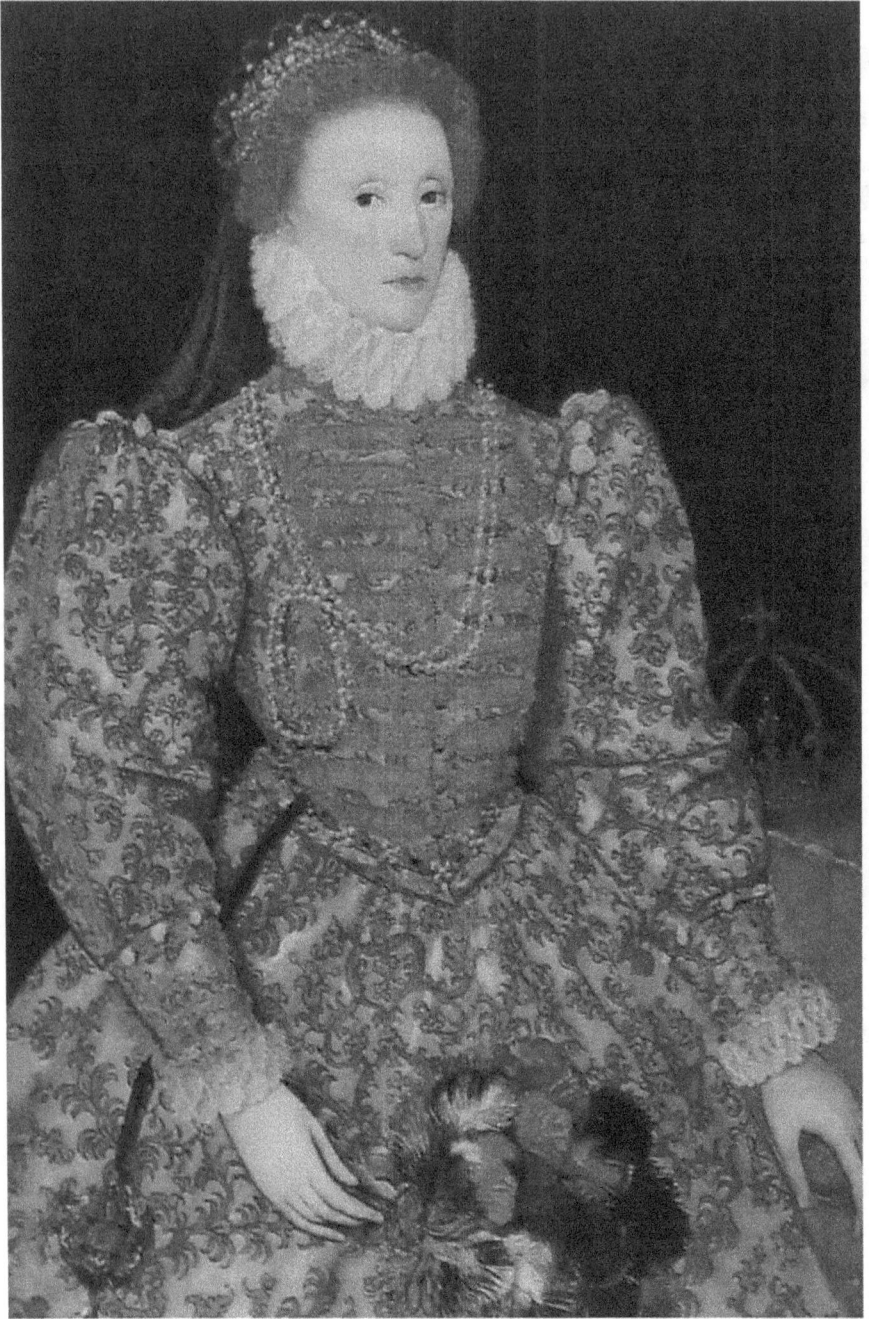

Elizabeth I, anonymous artist, 1575,
National Portrait Gallery, London

DIANA

DIANA

UNTO HER MAJESTY's SACRED HONOURABLE MAIDS

Eternal Twins! that conquer death and time,
Perpetual advocates in heaven and earth!
Fair, chaste, immaculate, and all divine,
Glorious alone, before the first man's birth;
Your twofold charities, celestial lights,
Bow your sun-rising eyes, planets of joy,
Upon these orphan poems; in whose rights
Conceit first claimed his birthright to enjoy.
If, pitiful, you shun the song of death,
Or fear the stain of love's life-dropping blood,
O know then, you are pure; and purer faith
Shall still keep white the flower, the fruit, and bud.
Love moveth all things. You that love, shall move
All things in him, and he in you shall love.

RICHARD SMITH

TO HIS MISTRESS

Grace full of grace, though in these verses here
My love complains of others than of thee,
Yet thee alone I loved, and they by me,
Thou yet unknown, only mistaken were.
Like him which feels a heat now here now there,
Blames now this cause now that, until he see
The fire indeed from whence they caused be;
Which fire I now do know is you, my dear,
Thus diverse loves dispersed in my verse
In thee alone for ever I unite,
And fully unto thee more to rehearse;
To him I fly for grace that rules above,
That by my grace I may live in delight,
Or by his grace I never more may love.

TO HIS ABSENT DIANA

Severed from sweet content, my live's sole light,
Banished by over-weening wit from my desire,
This poor acceptance only I require:
That though my fault have forced me from thy sight
Yet that thou would'st, my sorrows to requite,
Review these sonnets, pictures of thy praise;
Wherein each woe thy wondrous worth doth raise,
Though first thy worth bereft me of delight.
See them forsaken; for I them forsook,
Forsaken first of thee, next of my sense;
And when thou deign'st on their black tears to look,
Shed not one tear, my tears to recompence;
But joy in this, though fate 'gainst me repine,
My verse still lives to witness thee divine.

THE FIRST DECADE

I

Only of the birth and beginning of love

Resolved to love, unworthy to obtain,
I do no favour crave; but, humble wise,
To thee my sighs in verse I sacrifice,
Only some pity and no help to gain.
Hear then, and as my heart shall aye remain
A patient object to thy lightning eyes,
A patient ear bring thou to thund'ring cries;
Fear not the crack, when I the blow sustain.
So as thine eye bred mine ambitious thought,
So shall thine ear make proud my voice for joy.
Lo, dear, what wonders great by thee are wrought,
When I but little favour do enjoy!
The voice is made the ear for to rejoice,
And your ear giveth pleasure to my voice.

II

An excuse to his mistress for resolving to love so worthy a creature

Blame not my heart for flying up so high,
Sith thou art cause that it this flight begun;
For earthly vapours drawn up by the sun,
Comets become, and night suns in the sky.
Mine humble heart, so with thy heavenly eye
Drawn up aloft, all low desires doth shun;
Raise thou me up, as thou my heart hast done,
So during night in heaven remain may I.
I say again, blame not my high desire,
Sith of us both the cause thereof depends.
In thee doth shine, in me doth burn a fire,
Fire draws up other, and itself ascends.
Thine eye a fire, and so draws up my love;
My love a fire, and so ascends above.

III

Of the birth of his love

Fly low, dear love, thy sun dost thou not see?
Take heed, do not so near his rays aspire;
Lest, for thy pride, inflamed with wreakful ire,
It burn thy wings, as it hath burned me.
Thou haply sayst thy wings immortal be,
And so cannot consumed be with fire;
And one is hope, the other is desire,
And that the heavens bestowed them both on thee.
A muse's words made thee with hope to fly,
An angel's face desire hath begot,
Thyself engendered by a goddess' eye;
Yet for all this, immortal thou art not.
Of heavenly eye though thou begotten art,
Yet art thou born but of a mortal heart.

IV

Of his mistress, upon occasion of a friend of his which dissuaded him from loving

A friend of mine, pitying my hopeless love,
Hoping by killing hope my love to stay,
'Let not,' quoth he, 'thy hope, thy heart betray;
Impossible it is her heart to move.'
But sith resolved love cannot remove
As long as thy divine perfections stay,
Thy godhead then he sought to take away.
Dear, seek revenge and him a liar prove;
Gods only do impossibilities.
'Impossible,' saith he, 'thy grace to gain.'
Show then the power of divinities
By granting me thy favour to obtain.
So shall thy foe give to himself the lie;
A goddess thou shall prove, and happy I!

V

Of the conspiracy of his lady's eyes and his own to engender love

Thine eye the glass where I behold my heart,
Mine eye the window through the which thine eye
May see my heart, and there thyself espy
In bloody colours how thou painted art.
Thine eye the pile is of a murdering dart;
Mine eye the sight thou tak'st thy level by
To hit my heart, and never shoot'st awry.
Mine eye thus helps thine eye to work my smart.
Thine eye a fire is both in heat and light;
Mine eye of tears a river doth become.
O that the water of mine eye had might
To quench the flames that from thine eye doth come,
Or that the fires kindled by thine eye,
The flowing streams of mine eyes could make dry.

VI

Love's seven deadly sins

Mine eye with all the deadly sins is fraught.
First proud, sith it presumed to look so high.
A watchman being made, stood gazing by,
And idle, took no heed till I was caught.
And envious, bears envy that by thought
Should in his absence be to her so nigh.
To kill my heart, mine eye let in her eye;
And so consent gave to a murder wrought.
And covetous, it never would remove
From her fair hair, gold so doth please his sight.
Unchaste, a baud between my heart and love.
A glutton eye, with tears drunk every night.
These sins procured have a goddess' ire,
Wherefore my heart is damned in love's sweet fire.

VII

Of the slander envy gives him for so highly praising his mistress

Falsely doth envy of your praises blame
My tongue, my pen, my heart of flattery,
Because I said there was no sun but thee.
It called my tongue the partial trump of fame,
And saith my pen hath flattered thy name,
Because my pen did to my tongue agree;
And that my heart must needs a flatterer be,
Which taught both tongue and pen to say the same.
No, no, I flatter not when thee I call
The sun, sith that the sun was never such;
But when the sun thee I compared withal,
Doubtless the sun I flattered too much.
Witness mine eyes, I say the truth in this,
They have seen thee and know that so it is.

VIII

Of the end and death of his love

Much sorrow in itself my love doth move,
More my despair to love a hopeless bliss,
My folly most to love whom sure to miss
O help me, but this last grief to remove;
All pains, if you command, it joy shall prove,
And wisdom to seek joy. Then say but this,
'Because my pleasure in thy torment is,
I do command thee without hope to love!'
So when this thought my sorrow shall augment
That my own folly did procure my pain,
Then shall I say to give myself content,
'Obedience only made me love in vain.
It was your will, and not my want of wit;
I have the pain, bear you the blame of it!'

IX

Upon occasion of her walking in a garden

My lady's presence makes the roses red,
Because to see her lips they blush with shame.
The lily's leaves for envy pale became,
And her white hands in them this envy bred.
The marigold the leaves abroad doth spread,
Because the sun's and her power is the same.
The violet of purple colour came,
Dyed in the blood she made my heart to shed.
In brief, all flowers from her their virtue take;
From her sweet breath their sweet smells do proceed;
The living heat which her eyebeams doth make
Warmeth the ground and quickeneth the seed.
The rain wherewith she watereth the flowers,
Falls from mine eyes which she dissolves in showers.

X

To the Lady Rich

Heralds at arms do three perfections quote,
To wit, most fair, most rich, most glittering;
So when those three concur within one thing,
Needs must that thing of honour be a note.
Lately I did behold a rich fair coat,
Which wished fortune to mine eyes did bring.
A lordly coat, yet worthy of a king,
In which one might all these perfections note.
A field of lilies, roses proper bare;
Two stars in chief; the crest was waves of gold.
How glittering 'twas, might by the stars appear;
The lilies made it fair for to behold.
And rich it was as by the gold appeareth;
But happy he that in his arms it weareth!

THE SECOND DECADE

I

Of the end and death of his love

If true love might true love's reward obtain,
Dumb wonder only might speak of my joy;
But too much worth hath made thee too much coy,
And told me long ago I sighed in vain.
Not then vain hope of undeserved gain
Hath made me paint in verses mine annoy,
But for thy pleasure, that thou might'st enjoy
Thy beauty's praise, in glasses of my pain.
See then, thyself, though me thou wilt not hear,
By looking on my verse. For pain in verse,
Love doth in pain, beauty in love appear.
So if thou would'st my verses' meaning see,
Expound them thus, when I my love rehearse:
'None loves like he!' that is, 'None fair like me!'

II

How he encouraged himself to proceed in love, and to hope for
favour in the end at love's hands

It may be, love my death doth not pretend,
Although he shoots at me, but thinks it fit
Thus to bewitch thee for thy benefit,
Causing thy will to my wish to condescend.
For witches which some murder do intend,
Do make a picture and do shoot at it;
And in that part where they the picture hit,
The party's self doth languish to his end.
So love, too weak by force thy heart to taint,
Within my heart thy heavenly shape doth paint;
Suffering therein his arrows to abide,
Only to th'end he might by witches' art,
Within my heart pierce through thy picture's side,
And through thy picture's side might wound my heart.

III

Of the thoughts he nourished by night when she was retired to bed

The sun, his journey ending in the west,
Taketh his lodging up in Thetis' bed;
Though from our eyes his beams be banished,
Yet with his light th' antipodes be blest.
Now when the sun-time brings my sun to rest,
Which me too oft of rest hath hindered,
And whiter skin with white sheet covered,
And softer cheek doth on soft pillow rest,
Then I, O sun of suns! and light of lights!
Wish me with those antipodes to be,
Which see and feel thy beams and heat by nights.
Well, though the night both cold and darksome is,
Yet half the day's delight the night grants me,
I feel my sun's heat, though his light I miss.

IV

Of his lady's praise

Lady, in beauty and in favour rare,
Of favour, not of due, I favour crave.
Nature to thee beauty and favour gave;
Fair then thou art, and favour thou may'st spare.
Nor when on me bestowed your favours are,
Less favour in your face you shall not have;
If favour then a wounded soul may save,
Of murder's guilt, dear Lady, then beware.
My loss of life a million fold were less
Than the least loss should unto you befall;
Yet grant this gift; which gift when I possess,
Both I have life and you no loss at all.
For by your favour only I do live,
And favour you may well both keep and give.

V

Of the end and death of his love

My reason absent did mine eyes require
To watch and ward and such foes to descry
As they should ne'er my heart approaching spy;
But traitor eyes my heart's death did conspire,
Corrupted with hope's gifts; let in desire
To burn my heart; and sought no remedy,
Though store of water were in either eye,
Which well employed, might well have quenched the fire.
Reason returned; love and fortune made
Judges, to judge mine eyes to punishment.
Fortune, sith they by sight my heart betrayed
From wished sight, adjudged them banishment;
Love, sith by fire murdered my heart was found,
Adjudged them in tears for to be drowned.

VI

Of several complaints of misfortune in love only

Wonder it is and pity is't that she
In whom all beauty's treasure we may find,
That may unrich the body and the mind,
Towards the poor should use no charity.
My love has gone a begging unto thee.
And if that beauty had not been more kind
That pity, long ere this he had been pined;
But beauty is content his food to be.
O pity have when such poor orphans beg!
Love, naked boy, hath nothing on his back;
And though he wanteth neither arm nor leg,
Yet maimed he is sith he his sight doth lack.
And yet though blind he beauty can behold,
And yet though naked he feels more heat than cold.

VII

Of several complaints of misfortune in love only

Pity refusing my poor love to feed,
A beggar starved for want of help he lies;
And at your mouth, the door of beauty, cries,
That thence some alms of sweet grants might proceed.
But as he waiteth for some almes deed,
A cherry tree before the door he spies.
'O dear,' quoth he, 'two cherries may suffice.
Two only may save life in this my need.'
But beggars, can they nought but cherries eat?
Pardon my love, he is a goddess' son,
And never feedeth but on dainty meat,
Else need he not to pine, as he hath done;
For only the sweet fruit of this sweet tree
Can give food to my love and life to me.

VIII

Of his lady's veil wherewith she covered her

The fowler hides as closely as he may
The net, where caught the silly bird should be,
Lest he the threatening poison should but see,
And so for fear be forced to fly away.
My lady so, the while she doth assay
In curled knots fast to entangle me,
Put on her veil, to th' end I should not flee
The golden net wherein I am a prey.
Alas, most sweet! what need is of a net
To catch a bird that is already ta'en?
Sith with your hand alone you may it get,
For it desires to fly into the same.
What needs such art my thoughts then to entrap,
When of themselves they fly into your lap?

IX

To his lady's hand upon occasion of her glove which in her absence he kissed

Sweet hand, the sweet but cruel bow thou art,
From whence at me five ivory arrows fly;
So with five wounds at once I wounded lie,
Bearing my breast the print of every dart.
Saint Francis had the like, yet felt no smart,
Where I in living torments never die.
His wounds were in his hands and feet; where I
All these five helpless wounds feel in my heart.
Now, as Saint Francis, if a saint am I,
The bow that shot these shafts a relic is;
I mean the hand, which is the reason why
So many for devotion thee would kiss:
And some thy glove kiss as a thing divine,
This arrows' quiver, and this relic's shrine.

X

Of his lady's going over early to bed, so depriving him too soon of her sight

Fair sun, if you would have me praise your light,
When night approacheth wherefore do you fly?
Time is so short, beauties so many be,
As I have need to see them day and night,
That by continual view my verses might
Tell all the beams of your divinity;
Which praise to you and joy should be to me,
You living by my verse, I by your sight;
I by your sight, and not you by my verse,
Need mortal skill immortal praise rehearse?
No, no, though eyes were blind, and verse were dumb,
Your beauty should be seen and your fame known;
For by the wind which from my sighs do come,
Your praises round about the world are blown.

THE THIRD DECADE[1]

I

Complaint of his lady's sickness

Uncivil sickness, hast thou no regard,
But dost presume my dearest to molest,
And without leave dar'st enter in that breast
Whereto sweet love approach yet never dared?
Spare thou her health, which my life hath not spared;
Too bitter such revenge of my unrest!
Although with wrongs my thought she hath opprest,
My wrongs seek not revenge, they crave reward
Cease, sickness, cease in her then to remain;
And come and welcome, harbour thou in me
Whom love long since hath taught to suffer in!
So she which hath so oft my pain increased,
O God, that I might so revenged be,
By my poor pain might have her pain released!

---

1 Sonnets II to VIII were written by Sir Philip Sidney, and were published
in the *Arcadia* edition of 1598.

IX

Woe to mine eyes, the organs of mine ill;
Hate to my heart, for not concealing joy;
A double curse upon my tongue be still,
Whose babbling lost what else I might enjoy!
When first mine eyes did with thy beauty joy,
They to my heart thy wondrous virtues told;
Who, fearing lest thy beams should him destroy,
Whate'er he knew, did to my tongue unfold.
My tell-tale tongue, in talking over bold,
What they in private council did declare,
To thee, in plain and public terms unrolled;
And so by that made thee more coyer far.
What in thy praise he spoke, that didst thou trust;
And yet my sorrows thou dost hold unjust.

X

Of an Athenian young man have I read,
Who on blind fortune's picture doated so,
That when he could not buy it to his bed,
On it he gazing died for very woe.
My fortune's picture art thou, flinty dame,
That settest golden apples to my sight;
But wilt by no means let me taste the same.
To drown in sight of land is double spite.
Of fortune as thou learn'dst to be unkind,
So learn to be unconstant to disdain.
The wittiest women are to sport inclined.
Honour is pride, and pride is nought but pain.
Let others boast of choosing for the best;
'tis substances not names must make us blest.

THE FOURTH DECADE

I

Of the end and death of his love

Needs must I leave and yet needs must I love;
In vain my wit doth tell in verse my woe;
Despair in me, disdain in thee, doth show
How by my wit I do my folly prove.
All this my heart from love can never move.
Love is not in my heart. No, Lady, no,
My heart is love itself. Till I forego
My heart I never can my love remove.
How can I then leave love? I do intend
Not to crave grace, but yet to wish it still;
Not to praise thee, but beauty to commend;
And so, by beauty's praise, praise thee I will;
For as my heart is love, love not in me,
So beauty thou, beauty is not in thee.

II

Of the prowess of his lady

Sweet sovereign, since so many minds remain
Obedient subjects at thy beauty's call,
So many hearts bound in thy hairs as thrall,
So many eyes die with one look's disdain,
Go, seek the honour that doth thee pertain,
That the Fifth Monarchy may thee befall!
Thou hast such means to conquer men withal,
As all the world must yield or else be slain.
To fight, thou need'st no weapons but thine eyes,
Thine hair hath gold enough to pay thy men,
And for their food thy beauty will suffice;
For men and armour, Lady, care have none;
For one will sooner yield unto thee then
When he shall meet thee naked all alone.

III

Of the discouragement he had to proceed in love, through the
multitude of his lady's perfections and his own lowness

When your perfections to my thoughts appear,
They say among themselves, 'O happy we,
Whichever shall so rare an object see!'
But happy heart, if thoughts less happy were!
For their delights have cost my heart full dear,
In whom of love a thousand causes be,
And each cause breeds a thousand loves in me,
And each love more than thousand hearts can bear.
How can my heart so many loves then hold,
Which yet by heaps increase from day to day?
But like a ship that's o'ercharged with gold,
Must either sink or hurl the gold away.
But hurl not love; thou canst not, feeble heart;
In thine own blood, thou therefore drowned art!

IV

Fools be they that inveigh 'gainst Mahomet,
Who's but a moral of love's monarchy.
But a dull adamant, as straw by jet,
He in an iron chest was drawn on high.
In midst of Mecca's temple roof, some say,
He now hangs without touch or stay at all.
That Mahomet is she to whom I pray;
May ne'er man pray so ineffectual!
Mine eyes, love's strange exhaling adamants,
Un'wares, to my heart's temple's height have wrought
The iron idol that compassion wants,
Who my oft tears and travails sets at nought.
Iron hath been transformed to gold by art;
Her face, limbs, flesh and all, gold; save her heart.

V

Ready to seek out death in my disgrace,
My mistress 'gan to smooth her gathered brows,
Whereby I am reprieved for a space.
O hope and fear! who half your torments knows?
It is some mercy in a black-mouthed judge
To haste his prisoner's end, if he must die.
Dear, if all other favour you shall grudge,
Do speedy execution with your eye;
With one sole look you leave in me no soul!
Count it a loss to lose a faithful slave.
Would God, that I might hear my last bell toll,
So in your bosom I might dig a grave!
Doubtful delay is worse than any fever,
Or help me soon, or cast me off for ever!

VI

Of the end and death of his love

Each day, new proofs of new despair I find,
That is, new deaths. No marvel then, though I
Make exile my last help; to th'end mine eye
Should not behold the death to me assigned.
Not that from death absence might save my mind,
But that it might take death more patiently;
Like him, the which by judge condemned to die,
To suffer with more ease, his eyes doth blind.
Your lips in scarlet clad, my judges be,
Pronouncing sentence of eternal 'No!'
Despair, the hangman that tormenteth me;
The death I suffer is the life I have.
For only life doth make me die in woe,
And only death I for my pardon crave.

VII

The richest relic Rome did ever view
Was' Caesar's tomb; on which, with cunning hand,
Jove's triple honours, the three fair Graces, stand,
Telling his virtues in their virtues true.
This Rome admired; but dearest dear, in you
Dwelleth the wonder of the happiest land,
And all the world to Neptune's furthest strand,
For what Rome shaped hath living life in you.
Thy naked beauty, bounteously displayed,
Enricheth monarchies of hearts with love;
Thine eyes to hear complaints are open laid;
Thine eyes' kind looks requite all pains I prove;
That of my death I dare not thee accuse;
But pride in me that baser chance refuse.

VII♭

Why thus unjustly, say, my cruel fate,
Dost thou adjudge my luckless eyes and heart,
The one to live exiled from that sweet smart,
Where th' other pines, imprisoned without date?
My luckless eyes must never more debate
Of those bright beams that eased my love apart;
And yet my heart, bound to them with love's dart,
Must there dwell ever to bemoan my state.
O had mine eyes been suffered there to rest,
Often they had my heart's unquiet eased;
Or had my heart with banishment been blest,
Mine eye with beauty never had been pleased!
But since these cross effects hath fortune wrought,
Dwell, heart, with her; eyes, view her in my thought!

---

2 Sonnet number IX was written by Sir Philip Sidney.

X

Hope, like the hyaena, coming to be old,
Alters his shape, is turned into despair.
Pity my hoary hopes, Maid of clear mould!
Think not that frowns can ever make thee fair.
What harm is it to kiss, to laugh, to play?
Beauty's no blossom, if it be not used.
Sweet dalliance keeps the wrinkles long away;
Repentance follows them that have refused.
To bring you to the knowledge of your good,
I seek, I sue. O try and then believe!
Each image can be chaste that's carved of wood.
You show you live, when men you do relieve.
Iron with wearing shines; rust wasteth treasure.
On earth but love there is no other pleasure.

THE FIFTH DECADE

I

Ay me, poor wretch, my prayer is turned to sin!
I say, 'I love!' My mistress says ''tis lust!'
Thus most we lose where most we seek to win.
Wit will make wicked what is ne'er so just.
And yet I can supplant her false surmise.
Lust is a fire that for an hour or twain
Giveth a scorching blaze and then he dies;
Love a continual furnace doth maintain.
A furnace! Well, this a furnace may be called;
For it burns inward, yields a smothering flame,
Sighs which, like boiled lead's smoking vapour, scald.
I sigh apace at echo of sighs' name.
Long have I served; no short blaze is my love.
Hid joys there are that maids scorn till they prove.

II

I do not now complain of my disgrace,
O cruel fair one! fair with cruel crost;
Nor of the hour, season, time, nor place;
Nor of my foil, for any freedom lost;
Nor of my courage, by misfortune daunted;
Nor of my wit, by overweening struck;
Nor of my sense, by any sound enchanted;
Nor of the force of fiery-pointed hook;
Nor of the steel that sticks within my wound;
Nor of my thoughts, by worser thoughts defaced;
Nor of the life I labour to confound.
But I complain, that being thus disgraced,
Fired, feared, frantic, fettered, shot through, slain,
My death is such as I may not complain.

III

If ever sorrow spoke from soul that loves,
As speaks a spirit in a man possest,
In me her spirit speaks. My soul it moves,
Whose sigh-swoll'n words breed whirlwinds in my
                breast;
Or like the echo of a passing bell,
Which sounding on the water seems to howl;
So rings my heart a fearful heavy knell,
And keeps all night in consort with the owl.
My cheeks with a thin ice of tears are clad,
Mine eyes like morning stars are bleared and red.
What resteth then but I be raging mad,
To see that she, my cares' chief conduit-head,
When all streams else help quench my burning heart,
Shuts up her springs and will no grace impart.

IV

You secret vales, you solitary fields,
You shores forsaken and you sounding rocks!
If ever groaning heart hath made you yield,
Or words half spoke that sense in prison locks,
Then 'mongst night shadows whisper out my death.
That when myself hath sealed my lips from speaking,
Each tell-tale echo with a weeping breath,
May both record my truth and true love's breaking.
You pretty flowers that smile for summer's sake,
Pull in your heads before my wat'ry eyes
Do turn the meadows to a standing lake,
By whose untimely floods your glory dies!
For lo, mine heart, resolved to moistening air,
Feedeth mine eyes which double tear for tear.

V

His shadow to Narcissus well presented,
How fair he was by such attractive love!
So if thou would'st thyself thy beauty prove,
Vulgar breath-mirrors might have well contented,
And to their prayers eternally consented,
Oaths, vows and sighs, if they believe might move;
But more thou forc'st, making my pen approve
Thy praise to all, least any had dissented.
When this hath wrought, thou which before wert known
But unto some, of all art now required,
And thine eyes' wonders wronged, because not shown
The world, with daily orisons desired.
Thy chaste fair gifts, with learning's breath is blown,
And thus my pen hath made thy sweets admired.

VI

I am no model figure, or sign of care,
But his eternal heart's-consuming essence,
In whom grief's commentaries written are,
Drawing gross passion into pure quintessence,
Not thine eye's fire, but fire of thine eye's disdain,
Fed by neglect of my continual grieving,
Attracts the true life's spirit of my pain,
And gives it thee, which gives me no relieving.
Within thine arms sad elegies I sing;
Unto thine eyes a true heart love-torn lay I:
Thou smell'st from me the savours sorrows bring;
My tears to taste my truth to touch display I.
Lo thus each sense, dear fair one, I importune;
But being care, thou flyest me as ill fortune.

VII

But being care, thou flyest me as ill fortune;-
Care the consuming canker of the mind!
The discord that disorders sweet hearts' tune!
Th' abortive bastard of a coward mind!
The lightfoot lackey that runs post by death,
Bearing the letters which contain our end!
The busy advocate that sells his breath,
Denouncing worst to him, is most his friend!
O dear, this care no interest holds in me;
But holy care, the guardian of thy fair,
Thine honour's champion, and thy virtue's fee,
The zeal which thee from barbarous times shall bear,
This care am I; this care my life hath taken.
Dear to my soul, then leave me not forsaken!

VIII

Dear to my soul, then, leave, me not forsaken!
Fly not! My heart within thy bosom sleepeth;
Even from myself and sense I have betaken
Me unto thee for whom my spirit weepeth,
And on the shore of that salt teary sea,
Couched in a bed of unseen seeming pleasure,
Where in imaginary thoughts thy fair self lay;
But being waked, robbed of my life's best treasure,
I call the heavens, air, earth, and seas to hear
My love, my truth, and black disdained estate,
Beating the rocks with bellowings of despair,
Which still with plaints my words reverberate,
Sighing, 'Alas, what shall become of me?'
Whilst echo cries, 'What shall become of me?'

IX

Whilst echo cries, 'What shall become of me?'
And desolate, my desolations pity,
Thou in thy beauty's carack sitt'st to see
My tragic downfall, and my funeral ditty.
No timbrel, but my heart thou play'st upon,
Whose strings are stretched unto the highest key;
The diapason, love; love is the unison;
In love my life and labours waste away.
Only regardless to the world thou leav'st me,
Whilst slain hopes, turning from the feast of sorrow,
Unto despair, their king, which ne'er deceives me,
Captives my heart, whose black night hates the morrow,
And he in truth of my distressed cry
Plants me a weeping star within mine eye.

X

Prometheus for stealing living fire
From heaven's king, was judged eternal death;
In self-same flame with unrelenting ire
Bound fast to Caucasus' low foot beneath.
So I, for stealing living beauty's fire
Into my verse that it may always live,
And change his forms to shapes of my desire,
Thou beauty's queen, self sentence like dost give.
Bound to thy feet in chains of life I lie;
For to thine eyes I never dare aspire;
And in thy beauty's brightness do I fry,
As poor Prometheus in the scalding fire;
Which tears maintain as oil the lamp revives;
Only my succour in thy favour lies.

THE SIXTH DECADE

I

One sun unto my life's day gives true light.
One moon dissolves my stormy night of woes.
One star my fate and happy fortune shows.
One saint I serve, one shrine with vows I dight.
One sun transfix'd hath burnt my heart outright,
One moon opposed my love in darkness throws.
One star hath bid my thoughts my wrongs disclose.
Saints scorn poor swains, shrines do my vows no right.
Yet if my love be found a holy fire,
Pure, unstained, without idolatry,
And she nathless in hate of my desire,
Lives to repose her in my misery,
My sun, my moon, my star, my saint, my shrine,
Mine be the torment but the guilt be thine!

II

To live in hell, and heaven to behold;
To welcome life, and die a living death;
To sweat with heat, and yet be freezing cold;
To grasp at stars, and lie the earth beneath;
To treat a maze that never shall have end;
To burn in sighs, and starve in daily tears;
To climb a hill, and never to descend;
Giants to kill, and quake at childish fears;
To pine for food, and watch th' Hesperian tree;
To thirst for drink, and nectar still to draw;
To live accurs'd whom men hold blest to be,
And weep those wrongs which never creature saw:
If this be love, if love in these be founded,
My heart is love, for these in it are grounded.

III

A carver, having loved too long in vain,
Hewed out the portraiture of Venus' son
In marble rock, upon the which did rain
Small drizzling drops, that from a fount did run:
Imagining the drops would either wear
His fury out, or quench his living flame;
But when he saw it bootless did appear,
He swore the water did augment the same.
So I, that seek in verse to carve thee out,
Hoping thy beauty will my flame allay,
Viewing my verse and poems all throughout,
Find my will rather to my love obey,
That with the carver I my work do blame,
Finding it still th' augmenter of my flame.

IV

Astronomers the heavens do divide
Into eight houses, where the god remains;
All which in thy perfections do abide.
For in thy feet, the queen of silence reigns;
About thy waist Jove's messenger doth dwell,
Inchanting me as I thereat admire;
And on thy dugs the queen of love doth tell
Her godhead's power in scrolls of my desire;
Thy beauty is the world's eternal sun;
Thy favours force a coward's heart to dare,
And in thy hairs Jove and his riches won.
Thy frowns hold Saturn; thine's the fixed stars.
Pardon me then, divine, to love thee well,
Since thou art heaven, and I in heaven would dwell!

V

Weary of love, my thoughts of love complained,
Till reason told them there was no such power,
And bade me view fair beauty's richest flower,
To see if there a naked boy remained.
Dear, to thine eyes, eyes that my soul hath pained,
Thoughts turned them back in that unhappy hour
To see if love kept there his royal bower,
For if not there, then no place him contained.
There was he not, nor boy, nor golden bow;
Yet as thou turned thy chaste fair eye aside,
A flame of fire did from thine eyelids go,
Which burnt my heart through my sore wounded side;
Then with a sigh, reason made thoughts to cry,
'There is no god of love, save that thine eye!'

VI

Forgive me, dear, for thundering on thy name;
Sure 'tis thyself that shows my love distrest.
For fire exhaled in freezing clouds possessed,
Warring for way, makes all the heavens exclaim.
Thy beauty so, the brightest living flame,
Wrapt in my cloudy heart, by winter prest,
Scorning to dwell within so base a nest,
Thunders in me thy everlasting flame.
O that my heart might still contain that fire!
Or that the fire would always light my heart!
Then should'st thou not disdain my true desire,
Or think I wronged thee to reveal to my smart;
For as the fire through freezing clouds doth break,
So not myself but thou in me would'st speak.

VII

My heart mine eye accuseth of his death,
Saying his wanton sight bred his unrest;
Mine eye affirms my heart's unconstant faith
Hath been his bane, and all his joys repressed.
My heart avows mine eye let in the fire,
Which burns him with an everliving light.
Mine eye replies my greedy heart's desire
Let in those floods, which drown him day and night.
Thus wars my heart which reason doth maintain,
And calls my eye to combat if he dare,
The whilst my soul impatient of disdain,
Wrings from his bondage unto death more near;
Save that my love still holdeth him in hand;
A kingdom thus divided cannot stand!

VIII

Unhappy day, unhappy month and season,
When first proud love, my joys away adjourning,
Poured into mine eye to her eye turning
A deadly juice, unto my green thought's reason.
Prisoner I am unto the eye I gaze on;
Eternally my love's flame is in burning;
A mortal shaft still wounds me in my mourning;
Thus prisoned, burnt and slain, the spirit, soul and
                    reason.
What tides me then since these pains which annoy me,
In my despair are evermore increasing?
The more I love, less is my pain's releasing;
That cursed be the fortune which destroys me,
The hour, the month, the season, and the cause,
When love first made me thrall to lovers' laws.

IX

Love hath I followed all too long, nought gaining;
And sighed I have in vain to sweet what smarteth,
But from his brow a fiery arrow parteth,
Thinking that I should him resist not plaining.
But cowardly my heart submiss remaining,
Yields to receive what shaft thy fair eye darteth.
Well do I see thine eye my bale imparteth,
And that save death no hope I am detaining.
For what is he can alter fortune's sliding?
One in his bed consumes his life away,
Other in wars, another in the sea;
The like effects in me have their abiding;
For heavens avowed my fortune should be such,
That I should die by loving far too much.

X

My God, my God, how much I love my goddess,
Whose virtues rare, unto the heavens arise!
My God, my God, how much I love her eyes
One shining bright, the other full of hardness!
My God, my God, how much I love her wisdom,
Whose works may ravish heaven's richest maker!
Of whose eyes' joys if I might be partaker
Then to my soul a holy rest would come.
My God, how much I love to hear her speak!
Whose hands I kiss and ravished oft rekisseth,
When she stands wotless whom so much she blesseth.
Say then, what mind this honest love would break;
Since her perfections pure, withouten blot,
Makes her beloved of thee, she knoweth not?

THE SEVENTH DECADE

I

The first created held a joyous bower,
A flowering field, the world's sole wonderment,
High Paradise, from whence a woman's power
Enticed him to fall to endless banishment.
This on the banks of Euphrates did stand,
Till the first Mover, by his wondrous might,
Planted it in thine eyes, thy face, thy hands,
From whence the world receives his fairest light.
Thy cheeks contain choice flowers; thy eyes, two suns;
Thy hands, the fruit that no life blood can stain;
And in thy breath, that heavenly music wons,
Which, when thou speak'st, angels their voices strain.
As from the first thy sex exiled me,
So to this next let me be called by thee!

II

Fair grace of graces, muse of muses all,
Thou Paradise, thou only heaven I know!
What influence hath bred my hateful woe,
That I from thee and them am forced to fall?
Thou falled from me, from thee I never shall,
Although my fortunes thou hast brought so low;
Yet shall my faith and service with thee go,
For live I do, on heaven and thee to call.
Banish'd all grace, no graces with me dwell;
Compelled to muse, my muses from me fly;
Excluded heaven, what can remain but hell?
Exiled from paradise, in hate I lie,
Cursing my stars; albeit I find it true,
I lost all these when I lost love and you.

III

What viewed I, dear, when I thine eyes beheld?
Love in his glory? No, him Thyrsis saw,
And stood the boy, whilst he his darts did draw,
Whose painted pride to baser swains he telled.
Saw I two suns? That sight is seen but seld.
Yet can their brood that teach the holy law
Gaze on their beams, and dread them not a straw,
Where princely looks are by their eyes repelled.
What saw I then? Doubtless it was Amen,
Armed with strong thunder and a lightning's flame,
Who bridegroom like with power was riding then,
Meaning that none should see him when he came.
Yet did I gaze; and thereby caught the wound
Which burns my heart and keeps my body sound.

IV

When tedious much and over weary long,
Cruel disdain reflecting from her brow,
Hath been the cause that I endured such wrong
And rest thus discontent and weary now.
Yet when posterity in time to come,
Shall find th' uncancelled tenour of her vow,
And her disdain be then confessed of some,
How much unkind and long, I find it now,
O yet even then-though then will be too late
To comfort me; dead, many a day, ere then-
They shall confess I did not force her heart;
And time shall make it known to other men
That ne'er had her disdain made me despair,
Had she not been so excellently fair.

V

Had she not been so excellently fair,
My muse had never mourned in lines of woe;
But I did too inestimable weigh her,
And that's the cause I now lament me so.
Yet not for her contempt do I complain me:
Complaints may ease the mind, but that is all;
Therefore though she too constantly disdain me,
I can but sigh and grieve, and so I shall.
Yet grieve I not because I must grieve ever;
And yet, alas, waste tears away, in vain;
I am resolved truly to persever,
Though she persisteth in her old disdain.
But that which grieves me most is that I see
Those which most fair, the most unkindest be.

VI

Thus long imposed to everlasting plaining,
Divinely constant to the worthiest fair,
And moved by eternally disdaining,
Aye to persever in unkind despair:
Because now silence wearily confined
In tedious dying and a dumb restraint,
Breaks forth in tears from mine unable mind
To ease her passion by a poor complaint;
O do not therefore to thyself suggest
That I can grieve to have immured so long
Upon the matter of mine own unrest;
Such grief is not the tenour of my song,
That 'bide so zealously so bad a wrong.
My grief is this; unless I speak and plain me,
Thou wilt persever ever to disdain me.

VII

Thou wilt persever ever to disdain me;
And I shall then die, when thou will repent it.
O do not therefore from complaint restrain me,
And take my life from me, to me that lent it!
For whilst these accents, weepingly exprest
In humble lines of reverentest zeal,
Have issue to complaint from mine unrest,
They but thy beauty's wonder shall reveal;
And though the grieved muse of some other lover,
Whose less devotions knew but woes like mine,
Would rather seek occasion to discover
How little pitiful and how much unkind,
They other not so worthy beauties find.
O, I not so! but seek with humble prayer,
Means how to move th' unmercifullest fair.

VIII

As draws the golden meteor of the day
Exhaled matter from the ground to heaven,
And by his secret nature, there to stay
The thing fast held, and yet of hold bereaven;
So by th' attractive excellence and might,
Born to the power of thy transparent eyes,
Drawn from myself, ravished with thy delight,
Whose dumb conceits divinely sirenise,
Lo, in suspense of fear and hope upholden,
Diversely poised with passions that pain me,
No resolution dares my thoughts embolden,
Since 'tis not I, but thou that dost sustain me.
O if there's none but thou can work my woe,
Wilt thou be still unkind and kill me so?

IX

Wilt thou be still unkind and kill me so,
Whose humbled vows with sorrowful appeal
Do still persist, and did so long ago
Intreat for pity with so pure a zeal?
Suffice the world shall, for the world can say
How much thy power hath power, and what it can;
Never was victor-hand yet moved to slay
The rendered captive, or the yielding man.
Then, O, why should thy woman-thought impose
Death and disdain on him that yields his breath,
To free his soul from discontent and woes,
And humble sacrifice to a certain death?
O since the world knows what the power can do,
What were't for thee to save and love me too?

X

I meet not mine by others' discontent,
For none compares with me in true devotion;
Yet though my tears and sighs to her be spent,
Her cruel heart disdains what they do motion.
Yet though persisting in eternal hate,
To aggravate the cause of my complaining,
Her fury ne'er confineth with a date,
I will not cease to love, for her disdaining.
Such puny thoughts of unresolved ground,
Whose inaudacity dares but base conceit,
In me and my love never shall be found.
Those coward thoughts unworthy minds await.
But those that love well have not yet begun;
Persever ever and have never done!

THE EIGHTH DECADE

I

Persever ever and have never done,
You weeping accent of my weary song!
O do not you eternal passions shun,
But be you true and everlasting long!
Say that she doth requite you with disdain;
Yet fortified with hope, endure your fortune;
Though cruel now she will be kind again;
Such haps as those, such loves as yours importune.
Though she protests the faithfullest severity
Inexecrable beauty is inflicting,
Kindness in time will pity your sincerity,
Though now it be your fortune's interdicting.
For some can say, whose loves have known like passion,
'Women are kind by kind, and coy for fashion.'

II

Give period to my matter of complaining,
Fair wonder of our time's admiring eye,
And entertain no more thy long disdaining,
Or give me leave at last that I may die.
For who can live, perpetually secluded
From death to life, that loathes her discontent?
Lest by some hope seducively deluded,
Such thoughts aspire to fortunate event;
But I that now have drawn mal-pleasant breath
Under the burden of thy cruel hate,
O, I must long and linger after death,
And yet I dare not give my life her date;
For if I die and thou repent t' have slain me,
'twill grieve me more than if thou didst disdain me.

III

'Twill grieve me more than if thou didst disdain me,
That I should die; and thou, because I die so.
And yet to die, it should not know to pain me,
If cruel beauty were content to bid so.
Death to my life, life to my long despair
Prolonged by her, given to my love and days,
Are means to tell how truly she is fair,
And I can die to testify her praise.
Yet not to die, though fairness me despiseth,
Is cause why in complaint I thus persever;
Though death me and my love inparadiseth,
By interdicting me from her for ever.
I do not grieve that I am forced to die,
But die to think upon the reason why.

IV

My tears are true. Though others be divine,
And sing of wars and Troy's new rising frame,
Meeting heroic feet in every line,
That tread high measures in the scene of fame,
And I, though disaccustoming my muse,
And sing but low songs in an humble vein,
May one day raise my style as others use,
And turn Elizon to a higher strain.
When re-intombing from oblivious ages
In better stanzas her surviving wonder,
I may opposed against the monster rage
That part desert and excellence asunder;
That she though coy may yet survive to see,
Her beauty's wonder lives again in me.

V

Conclusion of the whole

Sometimes in verse I praised, sometimes in verse sighed;
No more shall pen with love and beauty mell,
But to my heart alone my heart shall tell
How unseen flames do burn it day and night,
Lest flames give light, light bring my love to sight,
And my love prove my folly to excel.
Wherefore my love burns like the fire of hell,
Wherein is fire and yet there is no light;
For if one never loved like me, then why
Skill-less blames he the thing he doth not know?
And he that so hath loved should favour show,
For he hath been a fool as well as I.
Thus shall henceforth more pain, more folly have;
And folly past, may justly pardon crave.

A CALCULATION UPON THE BIRTH OF AN HONOURABLE LADY'S DAUGHTER, BORN IN THE YEAR 1588 AND ON A FRIDAY

Fair by inheritance, whom born we see
Both in the wondrous year and on the day
Wherein the fairest planet beareth sway,
The heavens to thee this fortune doth decree!
Thou of a world of hearts in time shall be
A monarch great, and with one beauty's ray
So many hosts of hearts thy face shall slay,
As all the rest for love shall yield to thee,
But even as Alexander when he knew
His father's conquests wept, lest he should leave
No kingdom unto him for to subdue:
So shall thy mother thee of praise bereave;
So many hearts already she hath slain,
As few behind to conquer shall remain.

THE FOLLOWING SONNETS ARE FROM THE MANUSCRIPT, BUT ARE NOT IN INCLUDED IN THE 1594 EDITION

I

Of the sudden surprising of his heart, and how unawares he was caught

Delight in your bright eyes my death did breed,
As light and glittering weapons babes allure
To play with fire and sword, and so procure
Then to be burnt and hurt ere they take heed,
Thy beauty so hath made me burn and bleed;
Yet shall my ashes and my blood assure
Thy beauty's fame forever to endure;
For thy fame's life from my death doth proceed;
Because my heart to ashes burned giveth
Life to thy fame, thou right a phoenix art,
And like a pelican thy beauty liveth
By sucking blood out of my breast and heart.
Lo why with wonder we may thee compare
Unto the pelican and phoenix rare!

II

An exhortation to the reader to come and see his mistress's beauty

Eyes curious to behold what nature can create,
Come see, come see, and write what wonder you do see,
Causing by true report our next posterity
Curse fortune for that they were born too late!
Come then and come ye all, come soon lest that
The time should be too short and men too few should be;
For all be few to write her least part's history,
Though they should ever write and never write but that.
Millions look on her eyes, millions think on her wit,
Millions speak of her, millions write of her hand.
The whole eye on the lip I do not understand;
Millions too few to praise but some one part of it,
As either of her eye or lip or hand to write,
The light or black, the taste or red, the soft or white.

III

Of the excellency of his lady's voice

Lady of ladies, the delight alone
For which to heaven earth doth no envy bear;
Seeing and hearing thee, we see and hear
Such voice, such light, as never sung nor shone.
The want of heaven I grant yet we may moan,
Not for the pleasure of the angels there,
As though in face or voice they like thee were,
But that they many be, and thou but one.
The basest notes which from thy voice proceed,
The treble of the angels do exceed,
So that I fear their choir to beautify,
Lest thou to some in heaven shall sing and shine.
Lo, when I hear thee sing, the reason why
Sighs of my breast keep time with notes of thine!

IV

Of her excellency both in singing and instruments

Not that thy hand is soft, is sweet, is white,
Thy lips sweet roses, breast sweet lily is,
That love esteems these three the chiefest bliss
Which nature ever made for lips' delight;
But when these three to show their heavenly might
Such wonders do, devotion then for this
Commandeth us with humble zeal to kiss
Such things as work miracles in our sight.
A lute of senseless wood, by nature dumb,
Touched by thy hand doth speak divinely well;
And from thy lips and breast sweet tunes do come
To my dead heart, the which new life do give.
Of greater wonders heard we never tell
Than for the dumb to speak, the dead to live.

V

Of the envy others bear to his lady for the former perfections

When beauty to the world vouchsafes this bliss,
To show the one whose other there is not,
The whitest skins red blushing shame doth blot,
And in the reddest cheeks pale envy is.
The fair and foul come thus alike by this;
For when the sun hath our horizon got,
Venus herself doth shine no more, God wot,
Than the least star that takes the light from his.
The poor in beauty thus content remain
To see their jealous cause revenged in thee,
And their fair foes afflicted with like pain.
Lo, the clear proof of thy divinity;
For unto God is only due this praise
The highest to pluck down, the low to raise!

VI

To his mistress, upon occasion of a Petrarch he gave her, showing her the reason why the Italian commenters dissent so much in the exposition thereof

Miracle of the world! I never will deny
That former poets praise the beauty of their days;
But all those beauties were but figures of thy praise,
And all those poets did of thee but prophesy.
Thy coming to the world hath taught us to descry
What Petrarch's Laura meant, for truth the lip bewrays.
Lo, why th' Italians, yet which never saw thy rays,
To find out Petrarch's sense such forged glosses try!
The beauties which he in a veil enclosed beheld
But revelations were within his surest heart
By which in parables thy coming he foretold;
His songs were hymns of thee, which only now before
Thy image should be sung; for thou that goddess art
Which only we without idolatry adore.

VII

Complaint of misfortune in love only

Now, now I love indeed, and suffer more
In one day now then I did in a year;
Great flames they be which but small sparkles were,
And wounded now, I was but pricked before.
No marvel then, though more than heretofore
I weep and sigh; how can great wounds be there
Where moisture runs not out? and ever, where
The fire is great, of smoke there must be store.
My heart was hitherto but like green wood,
Which must be dried before it will burn bright;
My former love served but my heart to dry;
Now Cupid for his fire doth find it good:
For now it burneth clear, and shall give light
For all the world your beauty to espy.

VIII

Complaint of his lady's melancholiness

If that one care had our two hearts possessed,
Or you once (felt) what I long suffered,
Then should thy heart accuse in my heart's stead
The rigour of itself for mine unrest.
Then should thine arm upon my shoulder rest,
And weight of grief sway down thy troubled head;
Then should thy tears upon my sheet be shed,
And then thy heart should pant upon my breast.
But when that other cares thy heart do seize,
Alas, what succour gain I then by this,
But double grief for thine and mine unease?
Yet when thou see'st thy hurts to wound my heart,
And so art taught by me what pity is,
Perhaps thy heart will learn to feel my smart.

IX

Dear, though from me your gratious looks depart,
And of that comfort do myself bereave,
Which both I did deserve and did receive,
Triumph not over much in this my smart.
Nay, rather they which now enjoy thy heart
For fear just cause of mourning should conceive,
Lest thou inconstant shouldst their trust deceive
Which like unto the weather changing art.
For in foul weather birds sing often will
In hope of fair, and in fair time will cease,
For fear fair time should not continue still;
So they may mourn which have thy heart possessed
For fear of change, and hope of change may ease
Their hearts whom grief of change doth now molest.

X

If ever any justly might complain
Of unrequited service, it is I;
Change is the thanks I have for loyalty,
And only her reward is her disdain;
So as just spite did almost me constrain,
Through torment her due praises to deny,
For he which vexed is with injury
By speaking ill doth ease his heart of pain.
But what, shall torture make me wrong her name?
No, no, a pris'ner constant thinks it shame,
Though he (were) racked his first truth to gainsay.
Her true given praise my first confession is;
Though her disdain do rack me night and day,
This I confessed, and will deny in this.

LICIA

OR

POEMS OF LOVE IN HONOR OF
THE ADMIRABLE AND SINGULAR
VIRTUES OF HIS LADY, TO THE
IMITATION OF THE BEST LATIN
POETS AND OTHERS

BY

GILES FLETCHER

(1593)

TO LICIA

THE WISE, KIND, VIRTUOUS, AND FAIR

Bright matchless star, the honour of the sky,
From whose clear shine heaven's vault hath all his light,
I send these poems to your graceful eye;
Do you but take them, and they have their right.
I build besides a temple to your name,
Wherein my thoughts shall daily sing your praise;
And will erect an altar for the same,
Which shall your virtues and your honour raise.
But heaven the temple of your honour is,
Whose brasen tops your worthy self made proud;
The ground an altar, base for such a bliss
With pity torn, because I sighed so loud.
And since my skill no worship can impart,
Make you an incense of my loving heart.
Sad all alone not long I musing sat,
But that my thoughts compelled me to aspire,
A laurel garland in my hand I gat;
So the Muses I approached the nigher.
My suite was this, a poet to become,
To drink with them, and from the heavens be fed.
Phœbus denied, and sware there was no room,
Such to be poets as fond fancy led.
With that I mourned and sat me down to weep.
Venus she smiled, and smiling to me said,
"Come, drink with me, and sit thee still and sleep."
This voice I heard; and Venus I obeyed.
That poison sweet hath done me all this wrong,
For now of love must needs be all my song.

II

Weary was love and sought to take his rest,
He made his choice, upon a virgin's lap;
And slyly crept from thence unto her breast,
Where still he meant to sport him in his hap;
The virgin frowned like Phœbus in a cloud;
"Go pack, sir boy, here is no room for such,
My breast no wanton foolish boy must shroud."
This said, my love did give the wag a touch;
Then as the foot that treads the stinging snake
Hastes to be gone, for fear what may ensue,
So love my love was forced for to forsake,
And for more speed, without his arrows flew.

     "Pardon," he said, "For why? You seemed to me
     My mother Venus in her pride to be."

III

The heavens beheld the beauty of my queen,
And all amazed, to wonder thus began:
"Why dotes not Jove, as erst we all have seen,
And shapes himself like to a seemly man?
Mean are the matches which he sought before,
Like bloomless buds, too base to make compare,
And she alone hath treasured beauty's store,
In whom all gifts and princely graces are."
Cupid replied: "I posted with the sun
To view the maids that livèd in those days,
And none there was that might not well be won,
But she, most hard, most cold, made of delays."
    Heavens were deceived, and wrong they do esteem,
    She hath no heat, although she living seem.

IV

Love and my love did range the forest wild,
Mounted alike, upon swift coursers both.
Love her encountered, though he was a child.
"Let's strive," saith he, whereat my love was wroth,
And scorned the boy, and checked him with a smile.
"I mounted am, and armèd with my spear;
Thou art too weak, thyself do not beguile;
I could thee conquer if I naked were."
With this love wept, and then my love replied:
"Kiss me, sweet boy, so weep my boy no more."
Thus did my love, and then her force she tried;
Love was made ice, that fire was before.
    A kiss of hers, as I, poor soul, do prove,
    Can make the hottest freeze and coldest love.

V

Love with her hair my love by force hath tied,
To serve her lips, her eyes, her voice, her hand;
I smiled for joy, when I the boy espied
To lie unchained and live at her command.
She if she look, or kiss, or sing, or smile,
Cupid withal doth smile, doth sing, doth kiss,
Lips, hands, voice, eyes, all hearts that may beguile,
Because she scorns all hearts but only this.
Venus for this in pride began to frown
That Cupid, born a god, enthralled should be.
She in disdain her pretty son threw down,
And in his place, with love she chainèd me.
    So now, sweet love, though I myself be thrall,
    Not her a goddess, but thyself I call.

VI

My love amazed did blush herself to see,
Pictured by art, all naked as she was.
"How could the painter know so much by me,
Or art effect what he hath brought to pass?
It is not like he naked me hath seen,
Or stood so nigh for to observe so much."
No, sweet; his eyes so near have never been,
Nor could his hands by art have cunning such;
I showed my heart, wherein you printed were,
You, naked you, as here you painted are;
In that my love your picture I must wear,
And show't to all, unless you have more care.
    Then take my heart, and place it with your own;
    So shall you naked never more be known.

VII

Death in a rage assaulted once my heart
With love of her, my love that doth deny.
I scorned his force, and wished him to depart,
I heartless was, and therefore could not die.
I live in her, in her I placed my life,
She guides my soul, and her I honour must.
Nor is this life but yet a living strife,
A thing unmeet, and yet a thing most just.
Cupid enraged did fly to make me love,
My heart lay guarded with those burning eyes
The sparks whereof denied him to remove;
So conquered now, he like a captive lies;
    Thus two at once by love were both undone,
    My heart not loved, and armless Venus' son.

VIII

Hard are the rocks, the marble, and the steel,
The ancient oak with wind and weather tossed;
But you, my love, far harder do I feel
Than flint, or these, or is the winter's frost.
My tears too weak, your heart they cannot move;
My sighs, that rock, like wind it cannot rent;
Too tiger-like you swear you cannot love;
But tears and sighs you fruitless back have sent.
The frost too hard, not melted with my flame,
I cinders am, and yet you feel no heat.
Surpass not these, sweet love, for very shame,
But let my tears, my vows, my sighs entreat;
    Then shall I say as by trial find;
    These all are hard, but you, my love, are kind.

IX

Love was laid down, all weary fast asleep,
Whereas my love his armor took away;
The boy awaked, and straight began to weep,
But stood amazed, and knew not what to say.
"Weep not, my boy," said Venus to her son,
"Thy weapons none can wield, but thou alone;
Licia the fair, this harm to thee hath done,
I saw her here, and presently was gone;
She will restore them, for she hath no need
To take thy weapons where thy valour lies;
For men to wound the Fates have her decreed,
With favour, hands, with beauty, and with eyes."
    No, Venus, no: she scorns them, credit me;
    But robbed thy son that none might care for thee.

X

A painter drew the image of the boy,
Swift love, with wings all naked, and yet blind;
With bow and arrows, bent for to destroy;
I blamed his skill, and fault I thus did find:
"A needless task I see thy cunning take;
Misled by love, thy fancy thee betrayed;
Love is no boy, nor blind, as men him make,
Nor weapons wears, whereof to be affrayed;
But if thou, love, wilt paint with greatest skill
A love, a maid, a goddess, and a queen;
Wonder and view at Licia's picture still,
For other love the world hath never seen;
    For she alone all hope all comfort gives;
    Men's hearts, souls, all, led by her favour lives."

XI

In Ida vale three queens the shepherd saw,
Queens of esteem, divine they were all three,
A sight of worth. But I a wonder shaw,
Their virtues all in one alone to be.
Licia the fair, surpassing Venus' pride,
(The matchless queen, commander of the gods,
When drawn with doves she in her pomp doth ride)
Hath far more beauty, and more grace by odds
Juno, Jove's wife, unmeet to make compare,
I grant a goddess, but not half so mild;
Minerva wise, a virtue, but not rare;
Yet these are mean, if that my love but smiled.
    She them surpasseth, when their prides are full
    As far as they surpass the meanest trull.

XII

I wish sometimes, although a worthless thing,
Spurred by ambition, glad to aspire,
Myself a monarch, or some mighty king,
And then my thoughts do wish for to be higher.
But when I view what winds the cedars toss,
What storms men feels that covet for renown,
I blame myself that I have wished my loss,
And scorn a kingdom, though it give a crown.
Ah Licia, though the wonder of my thought,
My heart's content, procurer of my bliss,
For whom a crown I do esteem as naught,
As Asia's wealth, too mean to buy a kiss!
    Kiss me, sweet love, this favor do for me;
    Then crowns and kingdoms shall I scorn for thee.

XIII

Enamored Jove commanding did entreat
Cupid to wound my love, which he denied,
And swore he could not for she wanted heat
And would not love, as he full oft had tried.
Jove in a rage, impatient this to hear,
Replied with threats; "I'll make you to obey!"
Whereat the boy did fly away for fear
To Licia's eyes, where safe intrenched he lay.
Then Jove he scorned, and dared him to his face,
For now more safe than in the heavens he dwelled,
Nor could Jove's wrath do wrong to such a place
Where grace and honour have their kingdom held.
    Thus in the pride and beauty of her eyes
    The seely boy the greatest god defies.

XIV

My love lay sleeping, where birds music made,
Shutting her eyes, disdainful of the light;
The heat was great but greater was the shade
Which her defended from his burning sight.
This Cupid saw, and came a kiss to take,
Sucking sweet nectar from her sugared breath;
She felt the touch, and blushed, and did awake,
Seeing t'was love, which she did think was death,
She cut his wings and causèd him to stay,
Making a vow, he should not thence depart,
Unless to her the wanton boy could pay
The truest, kindest and most loving heart.
    His feathers still she usèd for a fan,
     Till by exchange my heart his feathers won.

XV

I stood amazed, and saw my Licia shine,
Fairer than Phœbus, in his brightest pride,
Set forth in colors by a hand divine,
Where naught was wanting but a soul to guide.
It was a picture, that I could descry,
Yet made with art so as it seemed to live,
Surpassing fair, and yet it had no eye,
Whereof my senses could no reason give.
With that the painter bid me not to muse;
"Her eyes are shut, but I deserve no blame;
For if she saw, in faith, it could not choose
But that the work had wholly been a flame," –
    Then burn me, sweet, with brightness of your eyes,
    That phœnix-like from thence I may arise.

XVI

Grant, fairest kind, a kiss unto thy friend!
A blush replied, and yet a kiss I had.
It is not heaven that can such nectar send
Whereat my senses all amazed were glad.
This done, she fled as one that was affrayed,
And I desired to kiss by kissing more;
My love she frowned, and I my kissing stayed,
Yet wished to kiss her as I did before.
Then as the vine the propping elm doth clasp,
Loath to depart till both together die,
So fold me, sweet, until my latest gasp,
That in thy arms to death I kissed may lie.
    Thus whilst I live for kisses I must call;
    Still kiss me, sweet, or kiss me not at all.

XVII

As are the sands, fair Licia, on the shore,
Or colored flowers, garlands of the spring,
Or as the frosts not seen, not felt before,
Or as the fruits that autumn forth doth bring;
As twinkling stars, the tinsel of the night,
Or as the fish that gallop in the seas;
As airs each part that still escapes our sight,
So are my sighs, controllers of my ease.
Yet these are such as needs must have an end,
For things finite none else hath nature done;
Only the sighs, which from my heart I send,
Will never cease, but where they first begun.
    Accept them, sweet, as incense due to thee;
    For you immortal made them so to be.

XVIII

I swear, fair Licia, still for to be thine,
By heart, by eyes, by what I held most dear;
Thou checked mine oath, and said: these were not mine,
And that I had no right by them to swear.
Then by my sighs, my passions, and my tears,
My vows, my prayers, my sorrow, and my love,
My grief, my joy, my hope, and hopeless fears,
My heart is thine, and never shall remove.
These are not thine, though sent unto thy view,
All else I grant, by right they are thine own;
Let these suffice that what I swear is true,
And more than this if that it could be known.
    So shall all these though troubles ease my grief;
    If that they serve to work in thee belief.

XIX

That time, fair Licia, when I stole a kiss,
From off those lips, where Cupid lovely laid,
I quaked for cold, and found the cause was this:
My life which loved, for love behind me staid.
I sent my heart my life for to recall,
But that was held, not able to return,
And both detained as captives were in thrall,
And judged by her, that both by sighs should burn.
Fair, burn them both, for that they were so bold,
But let the altar be within thy heart;
And I shall live because my life you hold,
You that give life, to every living part;
    A flame I took when as I stole the kiss;
    Take you my life, yet can I live with this.

XX

First did I fear, when first my love began;
Possessed in fits by watchful jealousy,
I sought to keep what I by favour won,
And brooked no partner in my love to be.
But tyrant sickness fed upon my love,
And spread his ensigns, dyed with colour white;
Then was suspicion glad for to remove,
And loving much did fear to lose her quite.
Erect, fair sweet, the colors thou didst wear;
Dislodge thy griefs; the short'ners of content;
For now of life, not love, is all my fear,
Lest life and love be both together spent.
    Live but, fair love, and banish thy disease,
    And love, kind heart, both where and whom thou please.

XXI

Licia my love was sitting in a grove,
Tuning her smiles unto the chirping songs,
But straight she spied where two together strove,
Each one complaining of the other's wrongs.
Cupid did cry lamenting of the harm;
Jove's messenger, thou wrong'st me too too far;
Use thou thy rod, rely upon the charm;
Think not by speech my force thou canst debar.
A rod, Sir boy, were fitter for a child,
My weapons oft and tongue and mind you took;
And in my wrong at my distress thou smiled,
And scorned to grace me with a loving look.
    Speak you, sweet love, for you did all the wrong
    That broke his arrows, and did bind his tongue.

XXII

I might have died before my life begun,
Whenas my father for his country's good
The Persian's favor and the Sophy won
And yet with danger of his dearest blood.
Thy father, sweet, whom danger did beset,
Escapèd all, and for no other end
But only this, that you he might beget,
Whom heavens decreed into the world to send.
Then father, thank thy daughter for thy life,
And Neptune praise that yielded so to thee,
To calm the tempest when the storms were rife,
And that thy daughter should a Venus be.
    I call thee Venus, sweet, but be not wroth;
    Thou art more chaste, yet seas did favor both.

XXIII

My love was masked, and armèd with a fan,
To see the sun so careless of his light,
Which stood and gazed, and gazing waxèd wan
To see a star himself that was more bright.
Some did surmize she hid her from the sun,
Of whom in pride she scorned for to be kissed,
Or feared the harm by him to others done.
But these the reason of this wonder missed,
Nor durst the sun, if that her face were bare
In greatest pride, presume to take a kiss.
But she more kind did show she had more care
Than with her eyes eclipse him of his bliss.
    Unmask you, sweet, and spare not; dim the sun;
    Your light's enough, although that his were done.

XXIV

Whenas my love lay sickly in her bed,
Pale death did post in hope to have a prey;
But she so spotless made him that he fled;
"Unmeet to die," she cried, and could not stay.
Back he retired, and thus the heavens he told;
"All things that are, are subject unto me,
Both towns, and men, and what the world doth hold;
But her fair Licia still immortal be."
The heavens did grant; a goddess she was made,
Immortal, fair, unfit to suffer change.
So now she lives, and never more shall fade;
In earth a goddess, what can be more strange?
    Then will I hope, a goddess and so near,
    She cannot choose my sighs and prayers but hear.

XXV

Seven are the lights that wander in the skies,
And at these seven, I wonder in my love.
So see the moon, how pale she doth arise,
Standing amazed, as though she durst not move;
So is my sweet much paler than the snow,
Constant her looks, these looks that cannot change.
Mercury the next, a god sweet-tongued we know,
But her sweet voice doth wonders speak more strange.
The rising Sun doth boast him of his pride,
And yet my love is far more fair than he.
The warlike Mars can wieldless weapons guide,
But yet that god is far more weak than she.
The lovely Venus seemeth to be fair,
But at her best my love is far more bright.
Saturn for age with groans doth dim the air,
Whereas my love with smiles doth give it light.
    Gaze at her brows, where heaven ingrafted is;
    Then sigh, and swear, there is no heaven but this.

XXVI

I live, sweet love, whereas the gentle wind
Murmurs with sport in midst of thickest boughs,
Where loving woodbine doth the harbor bind,
And chirping birds do echo forth my vows;
Where strongest elm can scarce support the vine,
And sweetest flowers enameled have the ground;
Where Muses dwell; and yet hereat repine
That on the earth so rare a place was found.
But winds delight, I wish to be content;
I praise the woodbine, but I take no joy;
I moan the birds that music thus have spent;
As for the rest, they breed but mine annoy.
    Live then, fair Licia, in this place alone;
    Then shall I joy though all of these were gone.

XXVII

The crystal stream wherein my love did swim,
Melted in tears as partners of my woe;
Her shine was such as did the fountain dim,
The pearl-like fountain whiter than the snow;
Then like perfume, resolvèd with a heat,
The fountain smoked, as if it thought to burn;
A wonder strange to see the cold so great,
And yet the fountain into smoke to turn.
I searched the cause, and found it to be this:
She touched the water, and it burned with love.
Now by her means it purchased hath that bliss,
Which all diseases quickly can remove.
    Then if by you these streams thus blessèd be,
    Sweet, grant me love, and be not worse to me.

XXVIII

In time the strong and stately turrets fall,
In time the rose and silver lilies die,
In time the monarchs captive are and thrall,
In time the sea and rivers are made dry;
The hardest flint in time doth melt asunder;
Still living fame in time doth fade away;
The mountains proud we see in time come under;
And earth for age we see in time decay;
The sun in time forgets for to retire
From out the east where he was wont to rise;
The basest thoughts we see in time aspire,
The basest thoughts we see in time aspire,
And greedy minds in time do wealth despise.
 Thus all, sweet fair, in time must have an end,
 Except thy beauty, virtues, and thy friend.

XXIX

Why died I not whenas I last did sleep?
O sleep too short that shadowed forth my dear!
Heavens, hear my prayers, nor thus me waking keep!
For this were heaven, if thus I sleeping were.
For in that dark there shone a princely light;
Two milk-white hills, both full of nectar sweet,
Her ebon thighs, the wonder of my sight,
Where all my senses with their objects meet, –
I pass these sports, in secret that are best,
Wherein my thoughts did seem alive to be;
We both did strive, and weary both did rest;
I kissed her still, and still she kissèd me.
    Heavens, let me sleep, and shows my senses feed,
    Or let me wake and happy be indeed!

XXX

Whenas my Licia sailèd in the seas,
Viewing with pride god Neptune's stately crown,
A calm she made, and brought the merchant ease,
The storm she stayed, and checked him with a frown.
Love at the stern sate smiling and did sing
To see how seas had learned for to obey;
And balls of fire into the waves did fling;
And still the boy full wanton thus did say: —
"Both poles we burnt whereon the world doth turn,
The round of heaven from earth unto the skies;
And now the seas we both intend to burn,
I with my bow, and Licia with her eyes."
  Then since thy force, heavens, earth, nor seas can move,
  I conquered yield, and do confess I love.

XXXI

Whenas her lute is tunèd to her voice,
The air grows proud for honour of that sound,
And rocks do leap to show how they rejoice
That in the earth such music should be found.
Whenas her hair more worth, more pale than gold,
Like silver thread lies wafting in the air,
Diana-like she looks, but yet more bold;
Cruel in chase, more chaste and yet more fair.
Whenas she smiles, the clouds for envy breaks;
She Jove in pride encounters with a check;
The sun doth shine for joy whenas she speaks;
Thus heaven and earth do homage at her beck.
    Yet all these graces, blots, not graces are,
    If you, my love, of love do take no care.

XXXII

Years, months, days, hours, in sighs I sadly spend;
I black the night wherein I sleepless toss;
I love my griefs yet wish them at an end;
Thus time's expense increaseth but my loss.
I musing stand and wonder at my love,
That in so fair should be a heart of steel;
And then I think my fancy to remove,
But then more painful I my passions feel;
Thus must I love, sweet fair, until I die,
And your unkindness doth my love increase.
I conquered am, I can it not deny;
My life must end, yet shall my love not cease.
    Then heavens, make Licia fair most kind to me,
    Or with my life my loss may finished be!

XXXIII

I wrote my sighs, and sent them to my love;
I praised that fair that none enough could praise;
But plaints nor praises could fair Licia move;
Above my reach she did her virtues raise,
And thus replied: "False Scrawl, untrue thou art,
To feign those sighs that nowhere can be found;
For half those praises came not from his heart
Whose faith and love as yet was never found.
Thy master's life, false Scrawl shall be thy doom;
Because he burns, I judge thee to the flame;
Both your attempts deserve no better room."
Thus at her word we ashes both became.
    Believe me, fair, and let my paper live;
    Or be not fair, and so me freedom give.

XXXIV

Pale are my looks, forsaken of my life,
Cinders my bones, consumèd with thy flame,
Floods are my tears, to end this burning strife,
And yet I sigh for to increase the same;
I mourn alone because alone I burn;
Who doubts of this, then let him learn to love;
Her looks cold ice into a flame can turn,
As I distressèd in myself do prove.
Respect, fair Licia, what my torments are;
Count but the tithe both of my sighs and tears;
See how my love doth still increase my care,
And care's increase my life to nothing wears.
    Send but a sigh my flame for to increase,
    Or lend a tear and cause it so to cease.

XXXV

Whenas I wish, fair Licia, for a kiss
From those sweet lips where rose and lilies strive,
Straight do mine eyes repine at such a bliss,
And seek my lips thereof for to deprive;
And seek my lips thereof for to deprive;
Whenas I seek to glut mine eyes by sight,
My lips repine and call mine eyes away;
Thus both contend to have each other's right,
And both conspire to work my full decay.
O force admired of beauty in her pride,
In whose each part such strange effects there be,
That all my forces in themselves divide,
And make my senses plainly disagree.
    If all were mine, this envy would be gone;
    Then grant me all, fair sweet, or grant me none!

XXXVI

Hear how my sighs are echoed of the wind;
See how my tears are pitied by the rain;
Feel what a flame possessèd hath my mind;
Taste but the grief which I possess in vain.
Then if my sighs the blustering winds surpass,
And wat'ry tears the drops of rain exceed,
And if no flame like mine nor is nor was,
Nor grief like that whereon my soul doth feed,
Relent, fair Licia, when my sighs do blow;
Yield at my tears, that flintlike drops consume;
Accept the flame that doth my incense show,
Allow the grief that is my heart's perfume.
> Thus sighs and tears, flame, grief shall plead for me;
> So shall I pray, and you a goddess be.

XXXVII

I speak, fair Licia, what my torments be,
But then my speech too partial do I find;
For hardly words can with those thoughts agree,
Those thoughts that swarm in such a troubled mind.
Then do I vow my tongue shall never speak
Nor tell my grief that in my heart doth lie;
But cannon-like, I then surcharged do break,
And so my silence worse than speech I try.
Thus speech or none, they both do breed my care;
I live dismayed, and kill my heart with grief;
In all respects my case alike doth fare
To him that wants, and dare not ask relief.
 Then you, fair Lucia, sovereign of my heart,
 Read to yourself my anguish and my smart.

XXXVIII

Sweet, I protest, and seal it with an oath:
I never saw that so my thoughts did please;
And yet content displeased I see them wroth
To love so much and cannot have their ease.
I told my thoughts, my sovereign made a pause,
Disposed to grant, but willing to delay;
They then repined, for that they knew no cause,
And swore they wished she flatly would say nay.
Thus hath my love, my thoughts with treason filled,
Thus hath my love, my thoughts with treason filled,
And 'gainst my sovereign taught them to repine.
So thus my treason all my thoughts hath killed,
And made fair Licia say she is not mine.
　　But thoughts too rash my heart doth now repent;
　　And as you please, they swear, they are content.

XXXIX

Fair matchless nymph, respect but what I crave;
My thoughts are true, and honour is my love;
I fainting die whom yet a smile might save;
You gave the wound, and can the hurt remove.
Those eyes like stars that twinkle in the night,
And cheeks like rubies pale in lilies dyed,
Those ebon hands that darting hath such might
That in my soul my love and life divide,
Accept the passions of a man possessed;
Let love be loved and grant me leave to live;
Disperse those clouds that darkened have my rest,
And let your heaven a sun-like smile but give!
    Then shall I praise that heaven for such a sun
    That saved my life, whenas my grief begun.

XL

My grief begun, fair saint, when first I saw
Love in those eyes sit ruling with disdain,
Whose sweet commands did keep a world in awe,
And caused them serve your favor to obtain.
I stood as one enchanted with a frown,
Yet smiled to see all creatures serve those eyes,
Where each with sighs paid tribute to that crown,
And thought them gracèd by your dumb replies.
But I, ambitious, could not be content
Till that my service more than sighs made known;
And for that end my heart to you I sent
To say and swear that, fair, it is your own.
    Then greater graces, Licia, do impart,
    Not dumb replies unto a speaking heart.

SONNET MADE UPON THE TWO TWINS, DAUGHTERS OF THE LADY MOLLINEUX, BOTH PASSING LIKE, AND EXCEEDING FAIR

Poets did feign that heavens a Venus had,
Matchless herself, and Cupid was her son;
Men sued to these, and of their smiles were glad,
By whom so many famous were undone.
Now Cupid mourns that he hath lost his might,
And that these two so comely are to see;
And Venus frowns because they have her right.
Yet both so like that both shall blameless be;
With heaven's two twins for godhead these may strive,
And rule a world with least part of a frown;
Fairer than these two twins are not alive,
Both conquering queens, and both deserve a crown.
    My thoughts presage, which time to come shall try,
    That thousands conquered for their love shall die.

XLI

If, aged Charon, when my life shall end,
I pass thy ferry and my waftage pay,
Thy oars shall fall, thy boat and mast shall rend,
And through the deep shall be a dry foot-way.
For why? My heart with sighs doth breathe such flame
That air and water both incensèd be,
The boundless ocean from whose mouth they came,
For from my heat not heaven itself is free.
Then since to me thy loss can be no gain,
Avoid thy harm and fly what I foretell.
Make thou thy love with me for to be slain,
That I with her and both with thee may dwell.
  Thy fact thus, Charon, both of us shall bless,
  Thou save thy boat and I my love possess.

XLII

For if alone thou think to waft my love,
Her cold is such as can the sea command,
And frozen ice shall let thy boat to move,
Nor can thy forces row it from the land.
But if thou friendly both at once shalt take,
Thyself mayst rest. For why? My sighs will blow.
Our cold and heat so sweet a thaw shall make,
As that thy boat without thy help shall row.
Then will I sit and glut me on those eyes
Wherewith my life my eyes could never fill.
Thus from my boat that comfort shall arise,
The want whereof my life and hope did kill.
    Together placed so thou her scorn shalt cross,
    Where if we part thy boat must suffer loss.

XLIII

Are those two stars, her eyes, my life's light gone,
By which my soul was freèd from all dark?
And am I left distressed to live alone,
Where none my tears and mournful tale shall mark?
Ah sun, why shine thy looks, thy looks like gold,
When horsemen brave thou risest in the east?
Ah Cynthia pale, to whom my griefs I told,
Why do you both rejoice both man and beast?
And I alone, alone that dark possess
By Licia's absence brighter than the sun,
Whose smiling light did ease my sad distress,
And broke the clouds, when tears like rain begun.
    Heavens, grant that light and so me waking keep,
    Or shut my eyes and rock me fast asleep!

XLIV

Cruel fair love, I justly do complain
Of too much rigor and thy heart unkind,
That for mine eyes thou hast my body slain,
And would not grant that I should favour find.
I looked, fair love, and you my love looked fair,
I sighed for love and you for sport did smile.
Your smiles were such as did perfume the air,
And this perfumèd did my heart beguile.
Thus I confess the fault was in mine eyes,
Begun with sighs and ended with a flame.
I for your love did all the world despise;
And in these poems honored have your name.
    Then let your love so with my fault dispense,
    That all my parts feel not mine eyes' offense.

XLV

There shone a comet, and it was full west.
My thoughts presagèd what it did portend;
I found it threatened to my heart unrest,
And might in time my joys and comfort end.
I further sought and found it was a sun,
Which day nor night did never use to set.
It constant stood when heavens did restless run,
And did their virtues and their forces let.
The world did muse and wonder what it meant,
A sun to shine and in the west to rise;
To search the truth, I strength and spirits spent;
At length I found it was my Licia's eyes.
    Now never after soul shall live in dark,
    That hath the hap this western sun to mark.

XLVI

If he be dead, in whom no heart remains,
Or lifeless be in whom no life is found;
If he do pine that never comfort gains,
And be distressed that hath his deadly wound;
Then must I die whose heart elsewhere is clad,
And lifeless pass the greedy worms to feed;
Then must I pine that never comfort had,
And be distressed whose wound with tears doth bleed.
Which if I do, why do I not wax cold?
Why rest I not like one that wants a heart?
Why move I still like him that life doth hold,
And sense enjoy both of my joy and smart?
    Like Niobe queen which made a stone did weep,
    Licia my heart dead and alive doth keep.

XLVII

Like Memnon's rock, touched with the rising sun
Which yields a sound and echoes forth a voice,
But when it's drowned in western seas is done,
And drowsy-like leaves off to make a noise;
So I, my love, enlightened with your shine,
A poet's skill within my soul I shroud,
A poet's skill within my soul I shroud,
Not rude like that which finer wits decline,
But such as Muses to the best allowed.
But when your figure and your shape is gone
I speechless am like as I was before;
Or if I write, my verse is filled with moan,
And blurred with tears by falling in such store.
    Then muse not, Licia, if my Muse be slack,
    For when I wrote I did thy beauty lack.

XLVIII

I saw, sweet Licia, when the spider ran
Within your house to weave a worthless web,
You present were and feared her with your fan,
So that amazèd speedily she fled.
She in your house such sweet perfumes did smell,
And heard the Muses with their notes refined,
Thus filled with envy, could no longer dwell,
But straight returned and at your house repined.
Then tell me, spider, why of late I saw
Thee lose thy poison, and thy bowels gone;
Did these enchant and keep thy limbs in awe,
And made thy forces to be small or none?
    No, no, thou didst by chance my Licia see,
    Who for her look Minerva seemed to thee.

XLIX

If that I die, fair Licia, with disdain,
Or heartless live surprisèd with thy wrong,
Then heavens and earth shall accent both my pain,
And curse the time so cruel and so long.
If you be kind, my queen, as you are fair,
And aid my thoughts that still for conquest strive,
Then will I sing and never more despair,
And praise your kindness whilst I am alive.
Till then I pay the tribute of my tears,
To move thy mercy and thy constant truth.
Respect, fair love, how these with sorrow wears
The truest heart unless it find some ruth.
    Then grace me, sweet, and with thy favor raise me,
    So shall I live and all the world shall praise thee.

L

Ah Licia, sigh and say thou art my own;
Nay, be my own, as you full oft have said.
So shall your truth unto the world be known,
And I resolved where now I am afraid.
And if my tongue eternize can your praise,
Or silly speech increase your worthy fame,
If ought I can, to heaven your worth can raise,
The age to come shall wonder at the same.
In this respect your love, sweet love, I told,
My faith and truth I vowed should be forever.
You were the cause if that I was too bold;
Then pardon this my fault or love me never.
    But if you frown I wish that none believe me,
    For slain with sighs I'll die before I grieve thee.

LI

When first the sun whom all my senses serve,
Began to shine upon this earthly round,
The heavens for her all graces did reserve,
That Pandor-like with all she might abound.
Apollo placed his brightness in her eyes,
His skill presaging and his music sweet.
Mars gave his force; all force she now defies;
Venus her smiles wherewith she Mars did meet;
Python a voice, Diana made her chaste,
Ceres gave plenty, Cupid lent his bow,
Thetis his feet, there Pallas wisdom placed.
With these she queen-like kept a world in awe.
    Yet all these honors deemèd are but pelf,
    For she is much more worthy of herself.

LII

O sugared talk, wherewith my thoughts do live!
O brows, love's trophy and my senses' shine!
O charming smiles, that death or life can give!
O heavenly kisses from a mouth divine!
O wreaths too strong, and trammels made of hair!
O pearls inclosèd in an ebon pale!
O rose and lilies in a field most fair,
Where modest white doth make the red seem pale!
O voice whose accents live within my heart!
O heavenly hand that more than Atlas holds!
O sighs perfumed, that can release my smart!
O happy they whom in her arms she folds!
    Now if you ask where dwelleth all this bliss,
    Seek out my love and she will tell you this.

AN ODE

Love, I repent me that I thought
My sighs and languish dearly bought.
For sighs and languish both did prove
That he that languished sighed for love.
Cruel rigor, foe to state,
Looks disdainful, fraught with hate,
I did blame, but had no cause;
Love hath eyes, but hath no laws.
She was sad and could not choose
To see me sigh and sit and muse.
We both did love and both did doubt
Least any should our love find out.
Our hearts did speak, by sighs most hidden;
This means was left, all else forbidden.
I did frown her love to try,
She did sigh and straight did cry.
Both of us did sighs believe,
Yet either grievèd friend to grieve.
I did look and then did smile;
She left sighing all that while.
Both were glad to see that change,
Things in love that are not strange.
Suspicion, foolish foe to reason,
Causèd me seek to find some treason.
I did court another dame,
False in love, it is a shame! –
She was sorry this to view,
Thinking faith was proved untrue.
Then she swore she would not love
One whom false she once did prove.
I did vow I never meant
From promise made for to relent.
The more I said the worse she thought,
My oaths and vows were deemed as naught.

"False," she said "how can it be,
To court another yet love me?
Crowns and love no partners brook;
If she be liked I am forsook.
Farewell, false, and love her still,
Your chance was good, but mine was ill.
No harm to you, but this I crave,
That your new love may you deceive,
And jest with you as you have done,
For light's the love that quickly won."
"Kind, and fair-sweet, once believe me;
Jest I did but not to grieve thee.
Court I did, but did not love;
All my speech was you to prove.
Words and sighs and what I spent,
In show to her, to you were meant.
Fond I was your love to cross;
Jesting love oft brings this loss.
Forget this fault, and love your friend,
Which vows his truth unto the end."
"Content," she said, "if this you keep."
Thus both did kiss, and both did weep.
For women long they cannot chide,
As I by proof in this have tried.

A DIALOGUE BETWIXT TWO SEA-NYMPHS DORIS AND GALATEA CONCERNING POLPHEMUS; BRIEFLY TRANSLATED OUT OF LUCIAN

The sea-nymphs late did play them on the shore,
And smiled to see such sport was new begun,
A strife in love, the like not heard before,
Two nymphs contend which had the conquest won.
Doris the fair with Galate did chide;
She liked her choice, and to her taunts replied.

DORIS

Thy love, fair nymph, that courts thee on this plain,
As shepherds say and all the world can tell,
Is that foul rude Sicilian Cyclop-swain;
A shame, sweet nymph, that he with thee should mell.

GALATEA

Smile not, fair Doris, though he foul do seem,
Let pass thy words that savour of disgrace;
He's worth my love, and so I him esteem,
Renowned by birth, and come of Neptune's race,
Neptune that doth the glassy ocean tame,
Neptune, by birth from mighty Jove which came.

DORIS

I grant an honour to be Neptune's child,
A grace to be so near with Jove allied.
But yet, sweet nymph, with this be not beguiled;
Where nature's graces are by looks decried,
So foul, so rough, so ugly as a clown,
And worse than this, a monster with one eye!
Foul is not gracèd, though it wear a crown,

But fair is beauty, none can that deny.

GALATEA

Nor is he foul or shapeless as you say,
Or worse; for that he clownish seems to be,
Rough, satyr-like, the better he will play,
And manly looks the fitter are for me.
His frowning smiles are gracèd by his beard,
His eye-light, sun-like, shrouded is in one.
This me contents, and others make afeard.
He sees enough, and therefore wanteth none.

DORIS

Nay, then I see, sweet nymph, thou art in love,
And loving, dotes; and doting, dost commend
Foul to be fair; this oft do lovers prove;
I wish him fairer, or thy love an end.

GALATEA

Doris, I love not, yet I hardly bear
Disgraceful terms, which you have spoke in scorn.
You are not loved; and that's the cause I fear;
For why? My love of Jove himself was born.
Feeding his sheep of late amidst this plain,
Whenas we nymphs did sport us on the shore,
He scorned you all, my love for to obtain;
That grieved your hearts; I knew as much before.
Nay, smile not, nymphs, the truth I only tell,
For few can brook that others should excel.

DORIS

Should I envy that blind did you that spite?
Or that your shape doth please so foul a groom?
The shepherd thought of milk, you looked so white;

The clown did err, and foolish was his doom.
Your look was pale, and so his stomach fed;
But far from fair, where white doth want his red.

GALATEA

Though pale my look, yet he my love did crave,
And lovely you, unliked, unloved I view;
It's better far one base than none to have;
Your fair is foul, to whom there's none will sue.
　　My love doth tune his love unto his harp.
　　His shape is rude, but yet his wit is sharp.

DORIS

Leave off, sweet nymph, to grace a worthless clown.
He itched with love, and then did sing or say;
The noise was such as all the nymphs did frown,
And well suspected that some ass did bray.
The woods did chide to hear this ugly sound
The prating echo scorned for to repeat;
This grisly voice did fear the hollow ground,
Whilst artless fingers did his harpstrings beat.
Two bear-whelps in his arms this monster bore,
With these new puppies did this wanton play;
Their skins was rough but yet your loves was more;
He fouler was and far more fierce than they.
I cannot choose, sweet nymph, to think, but smile
That some of us thou fear'st will thee beguile.

GALATEA

Scorn not my love, until it can be known
That you have one that's better of your own.

DORIS

I have no love, nor if I had, would boast;

Yet wooed have been by such as well might speed:
But him to love, the shame of all the coast,
So ugly foul, as yet I have no need.
  Now thus we learn what foolish love can do,
  To think him fair that's foul and ugly too.

To hear this talk, I sat behind an oak,
And marked their words and penned them as they spoke.

AD LECTOREM, DISTICHON

CUJUSDAM DE AUTORE

Lascivi quaeres fuerit cur carminis autor:
Carmine lascivus, mente pudicus erat.

A LOVER'S MAZE

True are my thoughts, my thoughts that are untrue,
Blind are my eyes, my eyes that are not blind,
New is my love, my love that is not new,
Kind is that fair, that fair that is not kind.
  Thus eyes and thoughts, that fairest fair, my love,
  Blind and untrue, unkind, unconstant prove.

True are my thoughts because they never flit,
Untrue my thoughts because they me betrayed;
Blind are my eyes because in clouds I sit,
Not blind my eyes because I looks obeyed.
  Thus eyes and thoughts, my dearest fair may view
  In sight, in love, not blind, nor yet untrue.

New is my love because it never dies,
Old is my love because it ever lives;
Kind is that fair because it hate denies,
Unkind that fair because no hope it gives.
  Thus new my love, and still that fair unkind,
  Renews my love, and I no favour find.

Sweet are my dreams, my dreams that are not sweet,
Long are the nights, the nights that are not long,
Meet are the pangs, these pangs that are unmeet,
Wronged is my heart, my heart that hath no wrong.
  Thus dreams, and night, my heart, my pangs, and all
  In taste, in length, conspire to work my fall.

Sweet are my dreams because my love they show,
Unsweet my dreams because but dreams they are;
Long are the nights because no help I know,
Meet are the nights because they end my care.
  Thus dreams and nights wherein my love take sport,
  Are sweet, unsweet, are long, and yet too short.

Meet are my pangs because I was too bold,
Unmeet my pangs because I loved so well;
Wronged was my heart because my grief it told,
Not wronged. For why? My grief it could not tell.
    Thus you my love unkindly cause this smart,
    That will not love to ease my pangs and heart.

Proud is her look, her look that is not proud,
Done all my days, my days that are not done,
Loud are my sighs, my sighs that are not loud,
Begun my death, my death not yet begun.
    Thus looks and days and sighs and death might move
    So kind, so fair, to give consent to love.

Proud is her look because she scorns to see,
Not proud her look for none dare say so much;
Done are my days because they hapless be,
Not done my days because I wish them such.
    Thus looks and days increase this loving strife.
    Not proud, nor done, nor dead, nor giving life.

Loud are my sighs because they pierce the sky,
Not loud my sighs because they are not heard;
My death begun because I artless cry,
But not begun because I am debarred.
    Thus sighs and death my heart no comfort give;
    Both life deny, and both do make me live.

Bold are her smiles, her smiles that are not bold,
Wise are her words, those words that are not wise,
Cold are her lips, those lips that are not cold,
Ice are those hands, those hands that are not ice.
    Thus smiles and words, her lips, her hands, and she,
    Bold, wise, cold, ice, love's cruel torments be.

Bold are her smiles, because they anger slay,
Not bold her smiles because they blush so oft;

✳ 162 ✳

Wise are her words because they wonders say,
Not wise her words because they are not soft.
    Thus smiles and words, so cruel and so bold,
    So blushing wise, my thoughts in prison hold.

Cold are her lips because they breathe no heat,
Not cold her lips because my heart they burn;
Ice are her hands because the snow's so great,
Not ice her hands that all to ashes turn.
    Thus lips and hands cold ice my sorrow brew;
    Hands, warm white snow and lips cold cherry-red.

Small was her waist, the waist that was not small,
Gold was her hair, the hair that was not gold,
Tall was her shape, the shape that was not tall;
Folding the arms, the arms that did not fold.
    Thus hair and shape, those folding arms and waist,
    Did make me love, and loving made me waste.

Small was her waist, because I could it span,
Not small her waist because she wanted all;
Gold was her hair because a crown it wan,
Not gold her hair because it was more pale.
    Thus smallest waist, the greatest waste doth make,
    And finest hair most fast a lover take.

Tall was her shape because she touched the sky,
Not tall her shape because she comely was;
Folding her arms because she hearts could tie,
Not folded arms because all bands they pass.
    Thus shape and arms with love my heart did ply,
    That hers I am, and must be till I die.

Sad was her joy, her joy that was not sad,
Short was her stay, her stay that was not short,
Glad was her speech, her speech that was not glad,
Sporting those toys, those toys that were not sport.
    Thus was my heart with joy, speech, toys and stay,

Possessed with love, and so stol'n quite away.

Sad was her joy because she did respect,
Not sad her joy because her joy she had,
Short was her stay because to small effect,
Long was her stay because I was so sad.
    Thus joy and stay, both crossed a lover's sport,
    The one was sad, the other too too short.

Glad was her speech because she spake her mind,
Not glad her speech because afraid to speak;
Sporting her toys because my love was kind,
Not toys in sport because my heart they break.
    Thus speech and toys my love began in jest;
    Sweet, yield to love, and make thy servant blest.

Tread you the maze, sweet love, that I have run,
Mark but the steps which I imprinted have;
End but your love whereas my thoughts begun;
So shall I joy and you a servant have.
    If not, sweet love, then this my suit deny;
    So shall you live, and so your servant die.

AN ELEGY

I

Down in a bed and on a bed of down,
Love, she, and I to sleep together lay;
She like a wanton kissed me with a frown,
Sleep, sleep, she said, but meant to steal away;
    I could not choose but kiss, but wake, but smile,
    To see how she thought us two to beguile.

She feigned a sleep, I waked her with a kiss;
A kiss to me she gave to make me sleep;
If I did wrong, sweet love, my fault was this,
In that I did not you thus waking keep.
    "Then kiss me, sweet, that so I sleep may take,
    Or let me kiss to keep you still awake."

The night drew on and needs she must be gone;
She wakèd Love, and bid him learn to wait;
She sighed, she said, to leave me there alone,
And bid Love stay but practise no deceit.
    Love wept for grief, and sighing made great moan,
    And could not sleep nor stay if she were gone.

"Then stay, sweet love;" a kiss with that I gave;
She could not stay, but gave my kiss again;
A kiss was all that I could get or crave,
And with a kiss she bound me to remain.
    "Ah Licia," still I in my dreams did cry,
    "Come, Licia, come, or else my heart will die."

II

Distance of place my love and me did part,
Yet both did swear we never would remove;
In sign thereof I bid her take my heart,
Which did, and doth, and can not choose but love.
    Thus did we part in hope to meet again,
    Where both did vow most constant to remain.

A she there was that passed betwixt us both,
By whom each knew how other's cause did fare;
For men to trust men in their love are loth;
Thus had we both of love a lover's care.
    Haply he seeks his sorrows to renew,
    That for his love doth make another sue.

By her a kiss, a kiss to me she sent.
A kiss for price more worth than purest gold.
She gave it her, to me the kiss was meant;
A she to kiss, what harm if she were bold?
    Happy those lips that had so sweet a kiss,
    For heaven itself scarce yields so sweet a bliss!

This modest she, blushing for shame of this,
Or loth to part from that she liked so well,
Did play false play, and gave me not the kiss;
Yet my love's kindness could not choose to tell.
    Then blame me not, that kissing sighed and swore
    I kissed but her whom you had kissed before.

Sweet, love me more, and blame me not, sweet love;
I kissed those lips, yet harmless I do vow;
Scarce would my lips from off those lips remove,
For still methought, sweet fair, I kissèd you.
    And thus, kind love, the sum of all my bliss
    Was but begun and ended in a kiss.

Then send me more, but send them by your friend;

Kiss none but her, nor her, nor none at all.
Beware by whom such treasures you do send,
I must them lose except I for them call.
    And love me, dear, and still still kissing be;
    Both like and love, but none, sweet love, but me.

III

If sad complaint would show a lover's pain,
Or tears express the torments of my heart,
If melting sighs would ruth and pity gain,
Or true laments but ease a lover's smart;

Then should my plaints the thunder's noise surmount,
And tears like seas should flow from out my eyes;
Then sighs like air should far exceed all count,
And true laments with sorrow dim the skies.

But plaints and tears, laments and sighs I spend,
Yet greater torments do my heart destroy;
I could all these from out my heart still send,
If after these I might my love enjoy.

But heavens conspire, and heavens I must obey,
That seeking love I still must want my ease;
For greatest joys are tempered with delay,
Things soon obtained do least of all us please.

My thoughts repine and think the time too long,
My love impatient wisheth to obtain;
I blame the heavens that do me all this wrong
To make me loved and will not ease my pain.

No pain like this, to love and not enjoy;
No grief like this, to mourn and not be heard;
No time so long as that which breeds annoy;

No hell like this, to love and be deferred!

But heaven shall stand and earth inconstant fly,
The sun shall freeze and ice inconstant burn,
The mountains flow and all the earth be dry,
Ere time shall force my loving thoughts to turn.

Do you resolve, sweet love, to do the same,
Say that you do, and seal it with a kiss.
Then shall our truths the heavens' unkindness blame
That can not hurt yet show their spite in this.

The silly 'prentice bound for many years,
Doth hope that time his service will release;
The town beseiged that lives in midst of fears,
Doth hope in time the cruel wars will cease.

The toiling plough-man sings in hope to reap,
The tosséd bark expecteth for a shore;
The boy at school to be at play doth leap,
And straight forgets the fear he had before.

If those by hope do joy in their distress,
And constant are in hope to conquer time,
Then let not hope in us, sweet friend, be less,
And cause our love to wither in the prime.

Let me conspire and time will have an end,
So both of us in time shall have a friend.

FINIS

FIDESSA

MORE CHASTE THAN KIND

BY

BARTHOLOMEW GRIFFIN

(1596)

TO FIDESSA

I

Fertur Fortunam Fortuna favere ferenti
    Fidessa fair, long live a happy maiden!
Blest from thy cradle by a worthy mother,
    High-thoughted like to her, with bounty laden,
Like pleasing grace affording, one and other;
    Sweet model of thy far renownèd sire!
Hold back a while thy ever-giving hand,
    And though these free penned lines do nought require,
For that they scorn at base reward to stand,
    Yet crave they most for that they beg the least
Dumb is the message of my hidden grief,
    And store of speech by silence is increased;
O let me die or purchase some relief!
    Bounteous Fidessa cannot be so cruel
As for to make my heart her fancy's fuel!

II

How can that piercing crystal-painted eye,
    That gave the onset to my high aspiring.
Yielding each look of mine a sweet reply,
    Adding new courage to my heart's desiring,
How can it shut itself within her ark,
    And keep herself and me both from the light,
Making us walk in all misguiding dark,
    Aye to remain in confines of the night?
How is it that so little room contains it,
    That guides the orient as the world the sun,
Which once obscured most bitterly complains it,
    Because it knows and rules whate'er is done?
The reason is that they may dread her sight,
Who doth both give and take away their light.

III

Venus, and young Adonis sitting by her,
    Under a myrtle shade, began to woo him;
She told the youngling how god Mars did try her,
    And as he fell to her, so fell she to him.
"Even thus," quoth she, "the wanton god embraced me!"
    And then she clasped Adonis in her arms;
"Even thus," quoth she, "the warlike god unlaced me!"
    As if the boy should use like loving charms.
But he, a wayward boy, refused the offer,
    And ran away the beauteous queen neglecting
Showing both folly to abuse her proffer,
    And all his sex of cowardice detecting.
O that I had my mistress at that bay,
To kiss and clip me till I ran away!

IV

Did you sometimes three German brethren see,
    Rancour 'twixt two of them so raging rife,
That th' one could stick the other with his knife?
    Now if the third assaulted chance to be
By a fourth stranger, him set on the three,
    Them two 'twixt whom afore was deadly strife
Made one to rob the stranger of his life;
    Then do you know our state as well as we.
Beauty and chastity with her were born,
    Both at one birth, and up with her did grow.
Beauty still foe to chastity was sworn,
    And chastity sworn to be beauty's foe;
And yet when I lay siege unto her heart,
Beauty and chastity both take her part.

V

Arraigned, poor captive at the bar I stand,
    The bar of beauty, bar to all my joys;
And up I hold my ever trembling hand,
    Wishing or life or death to end annoys.
And when the judge doth question of the guilt,
    And bids me speak, then sorrow shuts up words.
Yea, though he say, "Speak boldly what thou wilt!"
    Yet my confused affects no speech affords,
For why? Alas, my passions have no bound,
    For fear of death that penetrates so near;
And still one grief another doth confound,
    Yet doth at length a way to speech appear.
Then, for I speak too late, the Judge doth give
His sentence that in prison I shall live.

VI

Unhappy sentence, worst of worst of pains,
    To be in darksome silence, out of ken,
Banished from all that bliss the world contains,
    And thrust from out the companies of men!
Unhappy sentence, worse than worst of deaths,
    Never to see Fidessa's lovely face!
O better were I lose ten thousand breaths,
    Than ever live in such unseen disgrace!
Unhappy sentence, worse than pains of hell,
    To live in self-tormenting griefs alone;
Having my heart, my prison and my cell,
    And there consumed without relief to moan!
If that the sentence so unhappy be,
Then what am I that gave the same to me?

VII

Oft have mine eyes, the agents of mine heart,
    False traitor eyes conspiring my decay,
Pleaded for grace with dumb and silent art,
    Streaming forth tears my sorrows to allay;
Moaning the wrong they do unto their lord,
    Forcing the cruel fair by means to yield;
Making her 'gainst her will some grace t'afford,
    And striving sore at length to win the field;
Thus work they means to feed my fainting hope,
    And strengthened hope adds matter to each thought;
Yet when they all come to their end and scope
    They do but wholly bring poor me to nought.
She'll never yield although they ever cry,
And therefore we must all together die.

VIII

Grief-urging guest, great cause have I to plain me,
    Yet hope persuading hope expecteth grace,
And saith none but myself shall ever pain me;
    But grief my hopes exceedeth in this case;
For still my fortune ever more doth cross me
    By worse events than ever I expected;
And here and there ten thousand ways doth toss me,
    With sad remembrance of my time neglected.
These breed such thoughts as set my heart on fire,
    And like fell hounds pursue me to my death;
Traitors unto their sovereign lord and sire,
    Unkind exactors of their father's breath,
Whom in their rage they shall no sooner kill
Than they themselves themselves unjustly spill.

IX

My spotless love that never yet was tainted,
    My loyal heart that never can be moved,
My growing hope that never yet hath fainted,
    My constancy that you full well have proved,
All these consented have to plead for grace
    These all lie crying at the door of beauty; –
This wails, this sends out tears, this cries apace,
    All do reward expect of faith and duty;
Now either thou must prove th' unkindest one,
    And as thou fairest art must cruelest be,
Or else with pity yield unto their moan,
    Their moan that ever will importune thee.
Ah, thou must be unkind, and give denial,
And I, poor I, must stand unto my trial!

X

Clip not, sweet love, the wings of my desire,
    Although it soar aloft and mount too high:
But rather bear with me though I aspire,
    For I have wings to bear me to the sky.
What though I mount, there is no sun but thee!
    And sith no other sun, why should I fear?
Thou wilt not burn me, though thou terrify,
    And though thy brightness do so great appear.
Dear, I seek not to batter down thy glory,
    Nor do I envy that thy hope increaseth;
O never think thy fame doth make me sorry!
    For thou must live by fame when beauty ceaseth.
Besides, since from one root we both did spring,
Why should not I thy fame and beauty sing?

XI

Winged with sad woes, why doth fair zephyr blow
    Upon my face, the map of discontent?
Is it to have the weeds of sorrow grow
    So long and thick, that they will ne'er be spent?
No, fondling, no! It is to cool the fire
    Which hot desire within thy breast hath made.
Check him but once and he will soon retire.
    O but he sorrows brought which cannot fade!
The sorrows that he brought, he took from thee,
    Which fair Fidessa span and thou must wear!
Yet hath she nothing done of cruelty,
    But for her sake to try what thou wilt bear.
Come, sorrows, come! You are to me assigned;
I'll bear you all, it is Fidessa's mind.

XII

O if my heavenly sighs must prove annoy,
    Which are the sweetest music to my heart,
Let it suffice I count them as my joy,
    Sweet bitter joy and pleasant painful smart!
For when my breast is clogged with thousand cares,
    That my poor loaded heart is like to break,
Then every sigh doth question how it fares,
    Seeming to add their strength, which makes me weak;
Yet for they friendly are, I entertain them,
    And they too well are pleasèd with their host.
But I, had not Fidessa been, ere now had slain them;
    It's for her cause they live, in her they boast;
They promise help but when they see her face;
They fainting yield, and dare not sue for grace.

XIII

Compare me to the child that plays with fire,
    Or to the fly that dieth in the flame,
Or to the foolish boy that did aspire
    To touch the glory of high heaven's frame;
Compare me to Leander struggling in the waves,
    Not able to attain his safety's shore,
Or to the sick that do expect their graves,
    Or to the captive crying evermore;
Compare me to the weeping wounded hart,
    Moaning with tears the period of his life,
Or to the boar that will not feel the smart,
    When he is stricken with the butcher's knife;
No man to these can fitly me compare;
These live to die, I die to live in care.

XIV

When silent sleep had closèd up mine eyes,
    My watchful mind did then begin to muse;
A thousand pleasing thoughts did then arise,
    That sought by slights their master to abuse.
I saw, O heavenly sight! Fidessa's face,
    And fair dame nature blushing to behold it;
Now did she laugh, now wink, now smile apace,
    She took me by the hand and fast did hold it;
Sweetly her sweet body did she lay down by me;
    "Alas, poor wretch," quoth she, "great is thy sorrow;
But thou shall comfort find if thou wilt try me.
    I hope, sir boy, you'll tell me news to-morrow."
With that, away she went, and I did wake withal;
When ah! my honey thoughts were turned to gall.

XV

Care-charmer sleep! Sweet ease in restless misery!
 The captive's liberty, and his freedom's song!
Balm of the bruisèd heart! Man's chief felicity!
 Brother of quiet death, when life is too too long!
A comedy it is, and now an history;
 What is not sleep unto the feeble mind!
It easeth him that toils and him that's sorry;
 It makes the deaf to hear, to see the blind;
Ungentle sleep, thou helpest all but me!
 For when I sleep my soul is vexèd most.
It is Fidessa that doth master thee;
 If she approach, alas, thy power is lost!
But here she is! See how he runs amain!
I fear at night he will not come again.

XVI

For I have lovèd long, I crave reward;
  Reward me not unkindly, think on kindness;
Kindness becometh those of high regard;
  Regard with clemency a poor man's blindness;
Blindness provokes to pity when it crieth;
  It crieth "Give!" Dear lady, shew some pity!
Pity or let him die that daily dieth;
  Dieth he not oft who often sings this ditty?
This ditty pleaseth me although it choke me;
  Methinks dame Echo weepeth at my moaning,
Moaning the woes that to complain provoke me.
  Provoke me now no more, but hear my groaning,
Groaning both day and night doth tear my heart,
My heart doth know the cause and triumphs in the smart.

XVII

Sweet stroke, – so might I thrive as I must praise –
    But sweeter hand that gives so sweet a stroke!
The lute itself is sweetest when she plays.
    But what hear I? A string through fear is broke!
The lute doth shake as if it were afraid.
    O sure some goddess holds it in her hand,
A heavenly power that oft hath me dismayed,
    Yet such a power as doth in beauty stand!
Cease lute, my ceaseless suit will ne'er be heard!
    Ah, too hard-hearted she that will not hear it!
If I but think on joy, my joy is marred;
    My grief is great, yet ever must I bear it;
But love 'twixt us will prove a faithful page,
And she will love my sorrows to assuage.

XVIII

O she must love my sorrows to assuage.
    O God, what joy felt I when she did smile,
Whom killing grief before did cause to rage!
    Beauty is able sorrow to beguile.
Out, traitor absence! thou dost hinder me,
    And mak'st my mistress often to forget,
Causing me to rail upon her cruelty,
    Whilst thou my suit injuriously dost let;
Again her presence doth astonish me,
    And strikes me dumb as if my sense were gone;
Oh, is not this a strange perplexity?
    In presence dumb, she hears not absent moan;
Thus absent presence, present absence maketh,
That hearing my poor suit, she it mistaketh.

XIX

My pain paints out my love in doleful verse,
    The lively glass wherein she may behold it;
My verse her wrong to me doth still rehearse,
    But so as it lamenteth to unfold it.
Myself with ceaseless tears my harms bewail,
    And her obdurate heart not to be moved;
Though long-continued woes my senses fail,
    And curse the day, the hour when first I loved.
She takes the glass wherein herself she sees,
    In bloody colours cruelly depainted;
And her poor prisoner humbly on his knees,
    Pleading for grace, with heart that never fainted.
She breaks the glass; alas, I cannot choose
But grieve that I should so my labour lose!

XX

Great is the joy that no tongue can express!
    Fair babe new born, how much dost thou delight me!
But what, is mine so great? Yea, no whit less!
    So great that of all woes it doth acquite me.
It's fair Fidessa that this comfort bringeth,
    Who sorry for the wrongs by her procured,
Delightful tunes of love, of true love singeth,
    Wherewith her too chaste thoughts were ne'er inured.
She loves, she saith, but with a love not blind.
    Her love is counsel that I should not love,
But upon virtues fix a stayèd mind.
    But what! This new-coined love, love doth reprove?
If this be love of which you make such store,
Sweet, love me less, that you may love me more!

XXI

He that will Cæsar be, or else not be –
    Who can aspire to Cæsar's bleeding fame,
Must be of high resolve; but what is he
    That thinks to gain a second Cæsar's name?
Whoe'er he be that climbs above his strength,
    And climbeth high, the greater is his fall!
For though he sit awhile, we see at length,
    His slippery place no firmness hath at all,
Great is his bruise that falleth from on high.
    This warneth me that I should not aspire;
Examples should prevail; I care not, I!
    I perish must or have what I desire!
This humour doth with mine full well agree
I must Fidessa's be, or else not be!

XXII

It was of love, ungentle gentle boy!
    That thou didst come and harbour in my breast;
Not of intent my body to destroy,
    And have my soul, with restless cares opprest.
But sith thy love doth turn unto my pain,
    Return to Greece, sweet lad, where thou wast born.
Leave me alone my griefs to entertain,
    If thou forsake me, I am less forlorn;
Although alone, yet shall I find more ease.
    Then see thou hie thee hence, or I will chase thee;
Men highly wrongèd care not to displease;
    My fortune hangs on thee, thou dost disgrace me,
Yet at thy farewell, play a friendly part;
To make amends, fly to Fidessa's heart.

XXIII

Fly to her heart, hover about her heart,
    With dainty kisses mollify her heart,
Pierce with thy arrows her obdurate heart,
    With sweet allurements ever move her heart,
At midday and at midnight touch her heart,
    Be lurking closely, nestle about her heart,
With power – thou art a god! – command her heart,
    Kindle thy coals of love about her heart,
Yea, even into thyself transform her heart!
    Ah, she must love! Be sure thou have her heart;
And I must die if thou have not her heart;
    Thy bed if thou rest well, must be her heart;
He hath the best part sure that hath her heart;
What have I not, if I have but her heart!

XXIV

Striving is past! Ah, I must sink and drown,
    And that in sight of long descrièd shore!
I cannot send for aid unto the town,
    All help is vain and I must die therefore.
Then poor distressèd caitiff, be resolved
    To leave this earthly dwelling fraught with care;
Cease will thy woes, thy corpse in earth involved,
    Thou diest for her that will no help prepare.
O see, my case herself doth now behold;
    The casement open is; she seems to speak; –
But she has gone! O then I dare be bold
    And needs must say she caused my heart to break.
I die before I drown, O heavy case!
It was because I saw my mistress' face.

XXV

Compare me to Pygmalion with his image sotted,
    For, as was he, even so am I deceived.
The shadow only is to me allotted,
    The substance hath of substance me bereaved.
Then poor and helpless must I wander still
    In deep laments to pass succeeding days,
Welt'ring in woes that poor and mighty kill.
    O who is mighty that so soon decays!
The dread Almighty hath appointed so
    The final period of all worldly things.
Then as in time they come, so must they go;
    Death common is to beggars and to kings
For whither do I run beside my text?
I run to death, for death must be the next.

XXVI

The silly bird that hastes unto the net,
    And flutters to and fro till she be taken,
Doth look some food or succour there to get,
    But loseth life, so much is she mistaken.
The foolish fly that fleeth to the flame
    With ceaseless hovering and with restless flight,
Is burnèd straight to ashes in the same,
    And finds her death where was her most delight
The proud aspiring boy that needs would pry
    Into the secrets of the highest seat,
Had some conceit to gain content thereby,
    Or else his folly sure was wondrous great.
These did through folly perish all and die:
And though I know it, even so do I.

XXVII

Poor worm, poor silly worm, alas, poor beast!
    Fear makes thee hide thy head within the ground,
Because of creeping things thou art the least,
    Yet every foot gives thee thy mortal wound.
But I, thy fellow worm, am in worse state,
    For thou thy sun enjoyest, but I want mine.
I live in irksome night, O cruel fate!
    My sun will never rise, nor ever shine.
Thus blind of light, mine eyes misguide my feet,
    And baleful darkness makes me still afraid;
Men mock me when I stumble in the street,
    And wonder how my young sight so decayed.
Yet do I joy in this, even when I fall,
That I shall see again and then see all.

XXVIII

Well may my soul, immortal and divine,
    That is imprisoned in a lump of clay,
Breathe out laments until this body pine,
    That from her takes her pleasures all away.
Pine then, thou loathèd prison of my life,
    Untoward subject of the least aggrievance!
O let me die! Mortality is rife;
    Death comes by wounds, by sickness, care, and chance.
O earth, the time will come when I'll resume thee,
    And in thy bosom make my resting-place;
Then do not unto hardest sentence doom me;
    Yield, yield betimes; I must and will have grace!
Richly shalt thou be entombed, since, for thy grave,
Fidessa, fair Fidessa, thou shalt have!

XXIX

Earth, take this earth wherein my spirits languish;
    Spirits, leave this earth that doth in griefs retain you;
Griefs, chase this earth that it may fade with anguish;
    Spirits, avoid these furies which do pain you!
O leave your loathsome prison; freedom gain you;
    Your essence is divine; great is your power;
And yet you moan your wrongs and sore complain you,
    Hoping for joy which fadeth every hour.
O spirits, your prison loathe and freedom gain you;
    The destinies in deep laments have shut you
Of mortal hate, because they do disdain you,
    And yet of joy that they in prison put you.
Earth, take this earth with thee to be enclosed;
Life is to me, and I to it, opposed!

XXX

Weep now no more, mine eyes, but be you drowned
    In your own tears, so many years distilled.
And let her know that at them long hath frowned,
    That you can weep no more although she willed;
This hap her cruelty hath her allotten,
    Who whilom was commandress of each part;
That now her proper griefs must be forgotten
    By those true outward signs of inward smart.
For how can he that hath not one tear left him,
    Stream out those floods that are due unto her moaning,
When both of eyes and tears she hath bereft him?
    O yet I'll signify my grief with groaning;
True sighs, true groans shall echo in the air
And say, Fidessa, though most cruel, is most fair!

XXXI

Tongue, never cease to sing Fidessa's praise;
   Heart, however she deserve conceive the best;
Eyes, stand amazed to see her beauty's rays;
   Lips, steal one kiss and be for ever blest;
Hands, touch that hand wherein your life is closed;
   Breast, lock up fast in thee thy life's sole treasure;
Arms, still embrace and never be disclosed;
   Feet, run to her without or pace or measure;
Tongue, heart, eyes, lips, hands, breast, arms, feet,
   Consent to do true homage to your Queen,
Lovely, fair, gentle, wise, virtuous, sober, sweet,
   Whose like shall never be, hath never been!
O that I were all tongue, her praise to shew;
Then surely my poor heart were freed from woe!

XXXII

Sore sick of late, nature her due would have,
    Great was my pain where still my mind did rest;
No hope but heaven, no comfort but my grave,
    Which is of comforts both the last and least;
But on a sudden, the Almighty sent
    Sweet ease to the distressed and comfortless,
And gave me longer time for to repent,
    With health and strength the foes of feebleness;
Yet I my health no sooner 'gan recover,
    But my old thoughts, though full of cares, retained,
Made me, as erst, become a wretched lover
    Of her that love and lovers aye disdained.
Then was my pain with ease of pain increased,
And I ne'er sick until my sickness ceased.

XXXIII

He that would fain Fidessa's image see,
    My face of force may be his looking-glass.
There is she portrayed and her cruelty,
    Which as a wonder through the world must pass.
But were I dead, she would not be betrayed;
    It's I, that 'gainst my will, shall make it known.
Her cruelty by me must be bewrayed,
    Or I must hide my head and live alone.
I'll pluck my silver hairs from out my head,
    And wash away the wrinkles of my face;
Closely immured I'll live as I were dead,
    Before she suffer but the least disgrace.
How can I hide that is already known?
I have been seen and have no face but one.

XXXIV

Fie pleasure, fie! Thou cloy'st me with delight;
    Sweet thoughts, you kill me if you lower stray!
O many be the joys of one short night!
    Tush, fancies never can desire allay!
Happy, unhappy thoughts! I think, and have not.
    Pleasure, O pleasing pain! Shows nought avail me!
Mine own conceit doth glad me, more I crave not;
    Yet wanting substance, woe doth still assail me.
Babies do children please, and shadows fools;
    Shows have deceived the wisest many a time.
Ever to want our wish, our courage cools.
    The ladder broken, 'tis in vain to climb.
But I must wish, and crave, and seek, and climb;
It's hard if I obtain not grace in time.

XXXV

I have not spent the April of my time,
    The sweet of youth in plotting in the air,
But do at first adventure seek to climb,
    Whilst flowers of blooming years are green and fair.
I am no leaving of all-withering age,
    I have not suffered many winter lours;
I feel no storm unless my love do rage,
    And then in grief I spend both days and hours.
This yet doth comfort that my flower lasted
    Until it did approach my sun too near;
And then, alas, untimely was it blasted,
    So soon as once thy beauty did appear!
But after all, my comfort rests in this,
That for thy sake my youth decayèd is.

XXXVI

O let my heart, my body, and my tongue
    Bleed forth the lively streams of faith unfeigned,
Worship my saint the gods and saints among,
    Praise and extol her fair that me hath pained!
O let the smoke of my suppressed desire,
    Raked up in ashes of my burning breast,
Break out at length and to the clouds aspire,
    Urging the heavens to afford me rest;
But let my body naturally descend
    Into the bowels of our common mother,
And to the very centre let it wend,
    When it no lower can, her griefs to smother!
And yet when I so low do buried lie,
Then shall my love ascend unto the sky.

XXXVII

Fair is my love that feeds among the lilies,
    The lilies growing in that pleasant garden
Where Cupid's mount, that well beloved hill is,
    And where that little god himself is warden.
See where my love sits in the beds of spices,
    Beset all round with camphor, myrrh, and roses,
And interlaced with curious devices,
    Which her from all the world apart incloses.
There doth she tune her lute for her delight,
    And with sweet music makes the ground to move;
Whilst I, poor I, do sit in heavy plight,
    Wailing alone my unrespected love,
Not daring rush into so rare a place,
That gives to her, and she to it, a grace.

XXXVIII

Was never eye did see my mistress' face,
    Was never ear did hear Fidessa's tongue,
Was never mind that once did mind her grace,
    That ever thought the travail to be long.
When her I see, no creature I behold,
    So plainly say these advocates of love,
That now do fear and now to speak are bold,
    Trembling apace when they resolve to prove.
These strange effects do show a hidden power,
    A majesty all base attempts reproving,
That glads or daunts as she doth laugh or lower;
    Surely some goddess harbours in their moving
Who thus my Muse from base attempts hath raised,
Whom thus my Muse beyond compare hath praised.

XXXIX

My lady's hair is threads of beaten gold,
    Her front the purest crystal eye hath seen,
Her eyes the brightest stars the heavens hold,
    Her cheeks red roses such as seld have been;
Her pretty lips of red vermillion die,
    Her hand of ivory the purest white,
Her blush Aurora or the morning sky,
    Her breast displays two silver fountains bright
The spheres her voice, her grace the Graces three:
    Her body is the saint that I adore;
Her smiles and favours sweet as honey be;
    Her feet fair Thetis praiseth evermore.
But ah, the worst and last is yet behind,
For of a griffon she doth bear the mind!

XL

Injurious Fates, to rob me of my bliss,
    And dispossess my heart of all his hope!
You ought with just revenge to punish miss,
    For unto you the hearts of men are ope.
Injurious Fates, that hardened have her heart,
    Yet make her face to send out pleasing smiles!
And both are done but to increase my smart,
    And entertain my love with falsèd wiles.
Yet being when she smiles surprised with joy,
    I fain would languish in so sweet a pain,
Beseeching death my body to destroy,
    Lest on the sudden she should frown again.
When men do wish for death, Fates have no force;
But they, when men would live, have no remorse.

XLI

The prison I am in is thy fair face,
    Wherein my liberty enchainèd lies;
My thoughts, the bolts that hold me in the place;
    My food, the pleasing looks of thy fair eyes.
Deep is the prison where I lie enclosed,
    Strong are the bolts that in this cell contain me;
Sharp is the food necessity imposed,
    When hunger makes me feed on that which pains me.
Yet do I love, embrace, and follow fast,
    That holds, that keeps, that discontents me most;
And list not break, unlock, or seek to waste
    The place, the bolts, the food, though I be lost;
Better in prison ever to remain,
Than being out to suffer greater pain.

XLII

When never-speaking silence proves a wonder,
    When ever-flying flame at home remaineth,
When all-concealing night keeps darkness under,
    When men-devouring wrong true glory gaineth,
When soul-tormenting grief agrees with joy,
    When Lucifer foreruns the baleful night,
When Venus doth forsake her little boy,
    When her untoward boy obtaineth sight,
When Sisyphus doth cease to roll his stone,
    When Otus shaketh off his heavy chain,
When beauty, queen of pleasure, is alone,
    When love and virtue quiet peace disdain;
When these shall be, and I not be,
Then will Fidessa pity me.

XLIII

Tell me of love, sweet Love, who is thy sire,
    Or if thou mortal or immortal be?
Some say thou art begotten by desire,
    Nourished with hope, and fed with fantasy,
Engendered by a heavenly goddess' eye,
    Lurking most sweetly in an angel's face.
Others, that beauty thee doth deify; –
    O sovereign beauty, full of power and grace! –
But I must be absurd all this denying,
    Because the fairest fair alive ne'er knew thee.
Now, Cupid, comes thy godhead to the trying;
    'Twas she alone – such is her power – that slew me;
She shall be Love, and thou a foolish boy,
Whose virtue proves thy power is but a toy.

XLIV

No choice of change can ever change my mind;
    Choiceless my choice, the choicest choice alive;
Wonder of women, were she not unkind,
    The pitiless of pity to deprive.
Yet she, the kindest creature of her kind,
    Accuseth me of self-ingratitude,
And well she may, sith by good proof I find
    Myself had died, had she not helpful stood.
For when my sickness had the upper hand,
    And death began to show his awful face,
She took great pains my pains for to withstand,
    And eased my heart that was in heavy case.
But cruel now, she scorneth what it craveth;
Unkind in kindness, murdering while she saveth.

XLV

Mine eye bewrays the secrets of my heart,
    My heart unfolds his grief before her face;
Her face – bewitching pleasure of my smart! –
    Deigns not one look of mercy and of grace.
My guilty eye of murder and of treason, –
    Friendly conspirator of my decay,
Dumb eloquence, the lover's strongest reason! –
    Doth weep itself for anger quite away,
And chooseth rather not to be, than be
    Disloyal, by too well discharging duty;
And being out, joys it no more can see
    The sugared charms of all deceiving beauty.
But, for the other greedily doth eye it,
I pray you tell me, what do I get by it?

XLVI

So soon as peeping Lucifer, Aurora's star,
    The sky with golden periwigs doth spangle;
So soon as Phœbus gives us light from far,
    So soon as fowler doth the bird entangle;
Soon as the watchful bird, clock of the morn,
    Gives intimation of the day's appearing;
Soon as the jolly hunter winds his horn,
    His speech and voice with custom's echo clearing;
Soon as the hungry lion seeks his prey
    In solitary range of pathless mountains;
Soon as the passenger sets on his way,
    So soon as beasts resort unto the fountains;
So soon mine eyes their office are discharging,
And I my griefs with greater griefs enlarging.

XLVII

I see, I hear, I feel, I know, I rue
    My fate, my fame, my pain, my loss, my fall,
Mishap, reproach, disdain, a crown, her hue,
    Cruel, still flying, false, fair, funeral,
To cross, to shame, bewitch, deceive, and kill
    My first proceedings in their flowing bloom.
My worthless pen fast chainèd to my will,
    My erring life through an uncertain doom,
My thoughts that yet in lowliness do mount,
    My heart the subject of her tyranny;
What now remains but her severe account
    Of murder's crying guilt, foul butchery!
She was unhappy in her cradle breath,
That given was to be another's death.

XLVIII

"Murder! O murder!" I can cry no longer.
 "Murder! O murder!" Is there none to aid me?
Life feeble is in force, death is much stronger;
 Then let me die that shame may not upbraid me;
Nothing is left me now but shame or death.
 I fear she feareth not foul murder's guilt,
Nor do I fear to lose a servile breath.
 I know my blood was given to be spilt.
What is this life but maze of countless strays,
 The enemy of true felicity,
Fitly compared to dreams, to flowers, to plays!
 O life, no life to me, but misery!
Of shame or death, if thou must one,
Make choice of death and both are gone.

XLIX

My cruel fortunes clouded with a frown,
    Lurk in the bosom of eternal night;
My climbing thoughts are basely haulèd down;
    My best devices prove but after-sight.
Poor outcast of the world's exilèd room,
    I live in wilderness of deep lament;
No hope reserved me but a hopeless tomb,
    When fruitless life and fruitful woes are spent.
Shall Phœbus hinder little stars to shine,
    Or lofty cedar mushrooms leave to grow?
Sure mighty men at little ones repine,
    The rich is to the poor a common foe.
Fidessa, seeing how the world doth go,
Joineth with fortune in my overthrow.

L

When I the hooks of pleasure first devoured,
    Which undigested threaten now to choke me,
Fortune on me her golden graces showered;
    O then delight did to delight provoke me!
Delight, false instrument of my decay,
    Delight, the nothing that doth all things move,
Made me first wander from the perfect way,
    And fast entangled me in the snares of love.
Then my unhappy happiness at first began,
    Happy in that I loved the fairest fair;
Unhappily despised, a hapless man;
    Thus joy did triumph, triumph did despair.
My conquest is – which shall the conquest gain? –
Fidessa, author both of joy and pain!

LI

Work, work apace, you blessed sisters three,
    In restless twining of my fatal thread!
O let your nimble hands at once agree,
    To weave it out and cut it off with speed!
Then shall my vexèd and tormented ghost
    Have quiet passage to the Elysian rest,
And sweetly over death and fortune boast
    In everlasting triumphs with the blest.
But ah, too well I know you have conspired
    A lingering death for him that loatheth life,
As if with woes he never could be tired.
    For this you hide your all-dividing knife.
One comfort yet the heavens have assigned me;
That I must die and leave my griefs behind me.

LII

It is some comfort to the wrongèd man,
    The wronger of injustice to upbraid.
Justly myself herein I comfort can,
    And justly call her an ungrateful maid.
Thus am I pleased to rid myself of crime
    And stop the mouth of all-reporting fame,
Counting my greatest cross the loss of time
    And all my private grief her public shame.
Ah, but to speak the truth, hence are my cares,
    And in this comfort all discomfort resteth;
My harms I cause her scandal unawares;
    Thus love procures the thing that love detesteth.
For he that views the glasses of my smart
Must need report she hath a flinty heart.

LIII

I was a king of sweet content at least,
    But now from out my kingdom banished;
I was chief guest at fair dame pleasure's feast,
    But now I am for want of succour famished;
I was a saint and heaven was my rest,
    But now cast down into the lowest hell.
Vile caitiffs may not live among the blest,
    Nor blessed men amongst cursed caitiffs dwell.
Thus am I made an exile of a king;
    Thus choice of meats to want of food is changed;
Thus heaven's loss doth hellish torments bring;
    Self crosses make me from myself estranged.
Yet am I still the same but made another;
Then not the same; alas, I am no other!

LIV

If great Apollo offered as a dower
 His burning throne to beauty's excellence;
If Jove himself came in a golden shower
 Down to the earth to fetch fair Io thence;
If Venus in the curlèd locks was tied
 Of proud Adonis not of gentle kind;
If Tellus for a shepherd's favour died,
 The favour cruel Love to her assigned;
If Heaven's winged herald Hermes had
 His heart enchanted with a country maid;
If poor Pygmalion was for beauty mad;
 If gods and men have all for beauty strayed:
I am not then ashamed to be included
'Mongst those that love, and be with love deluded.

LV

O, No, I dare not! O, I may not speak!
    Yes, yes, I dare, I can, I must, I will!
Then heart, pour forth thy plaints and do not break;
    Let never fancy manly courage kill;
Intreat her mildly, words have pleasing charms
    Of force to move the most obdurate heart,
To take relenting pity of my harms,
    And with unfeignèd tears to wail my smart.
Is she a stock, a block, a stone, a flint?
    Hath she nor ears to hear nor eyes to see?
If so my cries, my prayers, my tears shall stint!
    Lord! how can lovers so bewitchèd be!
I took her to be beauty's queen alone;
But now I see she is a senseless stone.

LVI

Is trust betrayed? Doth kindness grow unkind?
    Can beauty both at once give life and kill?
Shall fortune alter the most constant mind?
    Will reason yield unto rebelling will?
Doth fancy purchase praise, and virtue shame?
    May show of goodness lurk in treachery?
Hath truth unto herself procurèd blame?
    Must sacred muses suffer misery?
Are women woe to men, traps for their falls?
    Differ their words, their deeds, their looks, their lives?
Have lovers ever been their tennis balls?
    Be husbands fearful of the chastest wives?
All men do these affirm, and so must I,
Unless Fidessa give to me the lie.

LVII

Three playfellows – such three were never seen
    In Venus' court – upon a summer's day,
Met altogether on a pleasant green,
    Intending at some pretty game to play.
They Dian, Cupid, and Fidessa were.
    Their wager, beauty, bow, and cruelty;
The conqueress the stakes away did bear.
    Whose fortune then was it to win all three?
Fidessa, which doth these as weapons use,
    To make the greatest heart her will obey;
And yet the most obedient to refuse
    As having power poor lovers to betray.
With these she wounds, she heals, gives life and death;
More power hath none that lives by mortal breath.

LVIII

O beauty, siren! kept with Circe's rod;
    The fairest good in seem but foulest ill;
The sweetest plague ordained for man by God,
    The pleasing subject of presumptuous will;
Th' alluring object of unstayèd eyes;
    Friended of all, but unto all a foe;
The dearest thing that any creature buys,
    And vainest too, it serves but for a show;
In seem a heaven, and yet from bliss exiling;
    Paying for truest service nought but pain;
Young men's undoing, young and old beguiling;
    Man's greatest loss though thought his greatest gain!
True, that all this with pain enough I prove;
And yet most true, I will Fidessa love.

LIX

Do I unto a cruel tiger play,
    That preys on me as wolf upon the lambs,
Who fear the danger both of night and day
    And run for succour to their tender dams?
Yet will I pray, though she be ever cruel,
    On bended knee and with submissive heart.
She is the fire and I must be the fuel;
    She must inflict and I endure the smart.
She must, she shall be mistress of her will,
    And I, poor I, obedient to the same;
As fit to suffer death as she to kill;
    As ready to be blamed as she to blame.
And for I am the subject of her ire,
All men shall know thereby my love entire.

LX

O let me sigh, weep, wail, and cry no more;
　　Or let me sigh, weep, wail, cry more and more!
Yea, let me sigh, weep, wail, cry evermore,
　　For she doth pity my complaints no more
Than cruel pagan or the savage Moor;
　　But still doth add unto my torments more,
Which grievous are to me by so much more
　　As she inflicts them and doth wish them more.
O let thy mercy, merciless, be never more!
　　So shall sweet death to me be welcome, more
Than is to hungry beasts the grassy moor,
　　As she that to affliction adds yet more,
Becomes more cruel by still adding more!
Weary am I to speak of this word "more;"
Yet never weary she, to plague me more!

LXI

Fidessa's worth in time begetteth praise;
　　Time, praise; praise, fame; fame, wonderment;
Wonder, fame, praise, time, her worth do raise
　　To highest pitch of dread astonishment.
Yet time in time her hardened heart bewrayeth
　　And praise itself her cruelty dispraiseth.
So that through praise, alas, her praise decayeth,
　　And that which makes it fall her honour raiseth!
Most strange, yet true! So wonder, wonder still,
　　And follow fast the wonder of these days;
For well I know all wonder to fulfil
　　Her will at length unto my will obeys.
Meantime let others praise her constancy,
And me attend upon her clemency.

LXII

Most true that I must fair Fidessa love.
    Most true that fair Fidessa cannot love.
Most true that I do feel the pains of love.
    Most true that I am captive unto love.
Most true that I deluded am with love.
    Most true that I do find the sleights of love.
Most true that nothing can procure her love.
    Most true that I must perish in my love.
Most true that she contemns the god of love.
    Most true that he is snarèd with her love.
Most true that she would have me cease to love.
    Most true that she herself alone is love.
Most true that though she hated, I would love.
Most true that dearest life shall end with love.

FINIS

Talis apud tales, talis sub tempore tali:
Subque meo tali judice, talis ero.

PHILLIS

HONORED WITH PASTORAL SONNETS,
ELEGIES, AND AMOROUS DELIGHTS

BY

THOMAS LODGE

(1595)

THE INDUCTION

I that obscured have fled the scene of fame,
Intitling my conceits to nought but care,
I that have lived a phœnix in love's flame,
And felt that death I never would declare,
    Now mount the theater of this our age,
    To plead my faith and Cupid's cursed rage.

Oh you high sp'rited paragons of wit,
That fly to fame beyond our earthly pitch,
Whose sense is sound, whose words are feat and fit,
Able to make the coyest ear to itch;
    Shroud with your mighty wings that mount so well,
    These little loves, new crept from out the shell.

And thou the true Octavia of our time,
Under whose worth beauty was never matched,
The genius of my muse and ragged rime,
Smile on these little loves but lately hatched,
    Who from the wrastling waves have made retreat,
    To plead for life before thy judgment seat.

And though the fore-bred brothers they have had,
Who in their swan-like songs Amintas wept,
For all their sweet-thought sighs had fortune bad,
And twice obscured in Cinthia's circle slept,
    Yet these I hope, under your kind aspect,
    Most worthy Lady, shall escape neglect.

And if these infants of mine artless brain,
Not by their worth but by thy worthiness,
A mean good liking of the learnèd gain,
My Muse enfranchised from forgetfulness
    Shall hatch such breed in honour of thy name,
    As modern poets shall admire the same.

As modern poets shall admire the same.
I mean not you (you never matchèd men)
Who brought the chaos of our tongue in frame,
Through these Herculean labours of your pen;
  I mean the mean, I mean no men divine,
  But such whose feathers are but waxed like mine.

Go, weeping truce-men in your sighing weeds,
Under a great Maecenas I have passed you;
If so you come where learnèd Colin feeds
His lovely flock, pack thence and quickly haste you;
  You are but mists before so bright a sun,
  Who hath the palm for deep invention won.

Kiss Delia's hand for her sweet prophet's sake,
Whose not affected but well couchèd tears
Have power, have worth, a marble mind to shake,
Whose fame no iron-age or time outwears.
  Then lay you down in Phillis' lap and sleep,
  Until the weeping read, and reading weep.

I

Oh pleasing thoughts, apprentices of love,
Fore-runners of desire, sweet mithridates
The poison of my sorrows to remove,
With whom my hopes and fear full oft debates!
    Enrich yourselves and me by your self riches,
Which are the thoughts you spend on heaven-bred beauty,
Rouse you my muse beyond our poets' pitches,
And, working wonders, yet say all is duty!
    Use you no eaglets' eyes, nor phœnix' feathers,
To tower the heaven from whence heaven's wonder sallies.
For why? Your sun sings sweetly to her weathers,
Making a spring of winter in the valleys.
    Show to the world though poor and scant my skill is
    How sweet thoughts be, that are but thought on
           Phillis!

II

You sacred sea-nymphs pleasantly disporting
Amidst this wat'ry world, where now I sail;
If ever love, or lovers sad reporting,
Had power sweet tears from your fair eyes to hail;
    And you, more gentle-hearted than the rest,
Under the northern noon-stead sweetly streaming,
Lend those moist riches of your crystal crest,
To quench the flames from my heart's Ætna streaming;
    And thou, kind Triton, in thy trumpet relish
The ruthful accents of my discontent,
That midst this travel desolate and hellish,
Some gentle wind that listens my lament
    May prattle in the north in Phillis' ears:
    "Where Phillis wants, Damon consumes in tears."

III

In fancy's world an Atlas have I been,
Where yet the chaos of my ceaseless care
Is by her eyes unpitied and unseen,
In whom all gifts but pity planted are;
    For mercy though still cries my moan-clad muse,
And every paper that she sends to beauty,
In tract of sable tears brings woeful news,
Of my true heart-kind thoughts, and loyal duty.
    But ah the strings of her hard heart are strained
Beyond the harmony of my desires;
And though the happy heavens themselves have pained,
To tame her heart whose will so far aspires,
    Yet she who claims the title of world's wonder,
    Thinks all deserts too base to bring her under.

IV

    Long hath my sufferance laboured to enforce
One pearl of pity from her pretty eyes,
Whilst I with restless rivers of remorse,
Have bathed the banks where my fair Phillis lies.
    The moaning lines which weeping I have written,
And writing read unto my ruthful sheep,
And reading sent with tears that never fitten,
To my love's queen, that hath my heart in keep,
    Have made my lambkins lay them down and sigh;
But Phillis sits, and reads, and calls them trifles.
Oh heavens, why climb not happy lines so high,
To rent that ruthless heart that all hearts rifles!
    None writes with truer faith, or greater love,
    Yet out, alas! I have no power to move.

V

Ah pale and dying infant of the spring,
How rightly now do I resemble thee!
That selfsame hand that thee from stalk did wring,
Hath rent my breast and robbed my heart from me.
    Yet shalt thou live. For why? Thy native vigour
Shall thrive by woeful dew-drops of my dolor;
And from the wounds I bear through fancy's rigour,
My streaming blood shall yield the crimson color.
    The ravished sighs that ceaseless take their issue
From out the furnace of my heart inflamed,
To yield you lasting springs shall never miss you;
So by my plaints and pains, you shall be famed.
    Let my heart's heat and cold, thy crimson nourish,
    And by my sorrows let thy beauty flourish.

VI

It is not death which wretched men call dying,
But that is very death which I endure,
When my coy-looking nymph, her grace envying,
By fatal frowns my domage doth procure.
    It is not life which we for life approve,
But that is life when on her wool-soft paps
I seal sweet kisses which do batten love,
And doubling them do treble my good haps.
    'Tis neither love the son, nor love the mother,
Which lovers praise and pray to; but that love is
Which she in eye and I in heart do smother.
Then muse not though I glory in my miss,
      Since she who holds my heart and me in durance,
      Hath life, death, love and all in her procurance.

VII

How languisheth the primrose of love's garden!
How trill her tears, th' elixir of my senses!
Ambitious sickness, what doth thee so harden?
Oh spare, and plague thou me for her offences!
    Ah roses, love's fair roses, do not languish;
Blush through the milk-white veil that holds you covered.
If heat or cold may mitigate your anguish,
I'll burn, I'll freeze, but you shall be recovered.
    Good God, would beauty mark now she is crased,
How but one shower of sickness makes her tender,
Her judgments then to mark my woes amazed,
To mercy should opinion's fort surrender!
    And I, – oh would I might, or would she meant it!
    Should hery love, who now in heart lament it.

VIII

No stars her eyes to clear the wandering night,
But shining suns of true divinity,
That make the soul conceive her perfect light!
No wanton beauties of humanity
    Her pretty brows, but beams that clear the sight
Of him that seeks the true philosophy!
No coral is her lip, no rose her fair,
    But even that crimson that adorns the sun.
No nymph is she, but mistress of the air,
By whom my glories are but new begun.
    But when I touch and taste as others do,
    I then shall write and you shall wonder too.

IX

The dewy roseate Morn had with her hairs
In sundry sorts the Indian clime adorned;
And now her eyes apparrelèd in tears,
The loss of lovely Memnon long had mourned,
    When as she spied the nymph whom I admire,
Combing her locks, of which the yellow gold
Made blush the beauties of her curlèd wire,
Which heaven itself with wonder might behold;
    Then red with shame, her reverend locks she rent,
And weeping hid the beauty of her face,
The flower of fancy wrought such discontent;
The sighs which midst the air she breathed a space,
    A three-days' stormy tempest did maintain,
    Her shame a fire, her eyes a swelling rain.

X

The rumour runs that here in Isis swim
Such stately swans so confident in dying,
That when they feel themselves near Lethe's brim,
They sing their fatal dirge when death is nighing.
    And I like these that feel my wounds are mortal,
Contented die for her whom I adore;
And in my joyful hymns do still exhort all
To die for such a saint or love no more.
    Not that my torments or her tyranny
Enforce me to enjoin so hard a task,
But for I know, and yield no reason why,
But will them try that have desire to ask.
    As love hath wreaths his pretty eyes to seel,
    So lovers must keep secret what they feel.

XI

My frail and earthly bark, by reason's guide,
Which holds the helm, whilst will doth wield the sail,
By my desires, the winds of bad betide,
Hath sailed these worldly seas with small avail,
    Vain objects serve for dreadful rocks to quail
My brittle boat from haven of life that flies
To haunt the sea of mundane miseries.
My soul that draws impressions from above,
    And views my course, and sees the winds aspire,
Bids reason watch to scape the shoals of love;
But lawless will enflamed with endless ire
Doth steer empoop, whilst reason doth retire.
    The streams increase; love's waves my bark do fill;
    Thus are they wracked that guide their course by will.

XII

Ah trees, why fall your leaves so fast?
Ah rocks, where are your robes of moss?
Ah flocks, why stand you all aghast?
Trees, rocks, and flocks, what, are you pensive for my loss?
    The birds methinks tune naught but moan,
The winds breathe naught but bitter plaint,
The beasts forsake their dens to groan;
Birds, winds, and beasts, what doth my loss your powers attaint?
    Floods weep their springs above their bounds,
And echo wails to see my woe,
The robe of ruth doth clothe the grounds;
Floods, echo, grounds, why do you all these tears bestow?
    The trees, the rocks, and flocks reply,
    The birds, the winds, the beasts report,
    Floods, echo, grounds, for sorrow cry,
We grieve since Phillis nill kind Damon's love consort.

XIII

Love guides the roses of thy lips,
And flies about them like a bee;
If I approach he forward skips,
And if I kiss he stingeth me.
    Love in thine eyes doth build his bower,
And sleeps within their pretty shine;
And if I look the boy will lower,
And from their orbs shoots shafts divine.
    Love works thy heart within his fire,
And in my tears doth firm the same;
And if I tempt it will retire,
And of my plaints doth make a game.
    Love, let me cull her choicest flowers,
And pity me, and calm her eye,
Make soft her heart, dissolve her lowers,
Then will I praise thy deity.
        But if thou do not love, I'll truly serve her
        In spite of thee, and by firm faith deserve her.

XIV

I wrote in Mirrha's bark, and as I wrote,
Poor Mirrha wept because I wrote forsaken;
'Twas of thy pride I sung in weeping note,
When as her leaves great moan for pity maken.
    The falling fountains from the mountains falling,
Cried out, alas, so fair and be so cruel!
And babbling echo never ceasèd calling,
Phillis, disdain is fit for none but truthless.
    The rising pines wherein I had engraved
Thy memory consulting with the wind,
Are trucemen to thy heart and thoughts depraved,
And say, thy kind should not be so unkind.
    But, out alas! so fell is Phillis fearless,
    That she hath made her Damon well nigh tearless.

XV

My Phillis hath the morning sun
At first to look upon her.
And Phillis hath morn-waking birds,
Her risings for to honour.
My Phillis hath prime-feathered flowers,
That smile when she treads on them,
And Phillis hath a gallant flock,
That leaps since she doth own them.
But Phillis hath so hard a heart –
Alas that she should have it! –
As yields no mercy to desert,
Nor grace to those that crave it.
Sweet sun, when thou look'st on,
Pray her regard my moan.
Sweet birds, when you sing to her,
To yield some pity woo her.
Sweet flowers, whenas she treads on,
Tell her, her beauty deads one.
And if in life her love she nill agree me,
Pray her before I die, she will come see me.

XVI

I part; but how? from joy, from hope, from life;
I leave; but whom? love's pride, wit's pomp, heart's bliss;
I pine; for what? for grief, for thought, for strife;
I faint; and why? because I see my miss.
    Oh ceaseless pains that never may be told,
    You make me weep as I to water would!
Ah weary hopes, in deep oblivious streams
Go seek your graves, since you have lost your grounds!
Ah pensive heart, seek out her radiant gleams!
For why? Thy bliss is shut within those bounds!
    All traitorous eyes, too feeble in for sight,
    Grow dim with woe, that now must want your light!
I part from bliss to dwell with ceaseless moan,
I part from life, since I from beauty part,
I part from peace, to pine in care alone,
I part from ease to die with dreadful smart.
I part – oh death! for why? this world contains
More care and woe than with despair remains.
    Oh loath depart, wherein such sorrows dwell,
    As all conceits are scant the same to tell!

XVII

Ah fleeting weal, ah sly deluding sleep,
That in one moment giv'st me joy and pain!
How do my hopes dissolve to tears in vain,
As wont the snows, 'fore angry sun to weep!
    Ah noisome life that hath no weal in keep!
My forward grief hath form and working might;
My pleasures like the shadows take their flight;
My path to bliss is tedious, long and steep.
    Twice happy thou Endymion that embracest
The live-long night thy love within thine arms,
Where thou fond dream my longèd weal defacest
Whilst fleeting and uncertain shades thou placest
Before my eyes with false deluding charms!
    Ah instant sweets which do my heart revive,
    How should I joy if you were true alive!

XVIII

As where two raging venoms are united,
Which of themselves dissevered life would sever,
The sickly wretch of sickness is acquited,
Which else should die, or pine in torments ever;
    So fire and frost, that hold my heart in seizure,
Restore those ruins which themselves have wrought,
Where if apart they both had had their pleasure,
The earth long since her fatal claim had caught.
    Thus two united deaths keep me from dying;
I burne in ice, and quake amidst the fire,
No hope midst these extremes or favour spying;
Thus love makes me a martyr in his ire.
      So that both cold and heat do rather feed
      My ceaseless pains, than any comfort breed.

XIX

Thou tyrannizing monarch that dost tire
My love-sick heart through those assaulting eyes,
That are the lamps which lighten my desire!
If nought but death thy fury may suffice,
　　Not for my peace, but for thy pleasure be it,
That Phillis, wrathful Phillis that repines me
All grace but death, may deign to come and see it,
And seeing grieve at that which she assigns me.
　　This only boon for all my mortal bane
I crave and cry for at thy mercy seat:
That when her wrath a faithful heart hath slain,
And soul is fled, and body reft of heat,
　　　　She might perceive how much she might command,
　　　　That had my life and death within her hand.

XX

Some praise the looks, and others praise the locks
Of their fair queens, in love with curious words;
Some laud the breast where love his treasure locks,
All like the eye that life and love affords.
    But none of these frail beauties and unstable
Shall make my pen riot in pompous style;
More greater gifts shall my grave muse enable,
Whereat severer brows shall never smile.
    I praise her honey-sweeter eloquence,
Which from the fountain of true wisdom floweth,
Her modest mien that matcheth excellence,
Her matchless faith which from her virtue groweth;
      And could my style her happy virtues equal,
      Time had no power her glories to enthral.

EGLOGA PRIMA DEMADES DAMON

DEMADES

Now scourge of winter's wrack is well nigh spent,
And sun gins look more longer on our clime,
And earth no more to sorrow doth consent,
Why been thy looks forlorn that view the prime?
 Unneth thy flocks may feed to see thee faint,
 Thou lost, they lean, and both with woe attaint.
For shame! Cast off these discontented looks;
For grief doth wait on life, though never sought;
So Thenot wrote admired for pipe and books.
Then to the spring attemper thou thy thought,
 And let advice rear up thy drooping mind,
 And leave to weep thy woes unto the wind.

DAMON

Ah Demades, no wonder though I wail,
For even the spring is winter unto me!
Look as the sun the earth doth then avail,
When by his beams her bowels warmèd be;
 Even so a saint more sun-bright in her shining
 First wrought my weal, now hastes my winter's pining.
Which lovely lamp withdrawn from my poor eyes,
Both parts of earth and fire drowned up in woe
In winter dwell. My joy, my courage dies;
My lambs with me that do my winter know
 For pity scorn the spring that nigheth near,
 And pine to see their master's pining cheer.
The root which yieldeth sap unto the tree
Draws from the earth the means that make it spring;
And by the sap the scions fostered be,
All from the sun have comfort and increasing
 And that fair eye that lights this earthly ball

Kills by depart, and nearing cheereth all.
As root to tree, such is my tender heart,
Whose sap is thought, whose branches are content;
And from my soul they draw their sweet or smart,
And from her eye, my soul's best life is lent;
Which heavenly eye that lights both earth and air,
Quells by depart and quickens by repair.

DEMADES

Give period to the process of thy plaint,
Unhappy Damon, witty in self-grieving;
Tend thou thy flocks; let tyrant love attaint
Those tender hearts that made their love their living.
    And as kind time keeps Phillis from thy sight,
    So let prevention banish fancy quite.

Cast hence this idle fuel of desire,
That feeds that flame wherein thy heart consumeth;
Let reason school thy will which doth aspire,
And counsel cool impatience that presumeth;
    Drive hence vain thoughts which are fond love's abettors,
    For he that seeks his thraldom merits fetters.

The vain idea of this deity
Nursed at the teat of thine imagination,
Was bred, brought up by thine own vanity,
Whose being thou mayst curse from the creation;
    And so thou list, thou may as soon forget love,
    As thou at first didst fashion and beget love.

DAMON

Peace, Demades, peace shepherd, do not tempt me;
The sage-taught wife may speak thus, but not practise;
Rather from life than from my love exempt me,
My happy love wherein my weal and wrack lies;
    Where chilly age first left love, and first lost her,

There youth found love, liked love, and love did foster.

Not as ambitious of their own decay,
But curious to equal your fore-deeds,
So tread we now within your wonted way;
We find your fruits of judgments and their seeds;
    We know you loved, and loving learn that lore;
    You scorn kind love, because you can no more.

Though from this pure refiner of the thought
The gleanings of your learnings have you gathered
Your lives had been abortive, base and naught,
Except by happy love they had been fathered;
    Then still the swain, for I will still avow it;
    They have no wit nor worth that disallow it.

Then to renew the ruins of my tears
Be thou no hinderer, Demades, I pray thee.
If my love-sighs grow tedious in thine ears,
Fly me, that fly from joy, I list not stay thee.
    Mourn sheep, mourn lambs, and Damon will weep by you;
    And when I sigh, "Come home, sweet Phillis," cry you.

Come home, sweet Phillis, for thine absence causeth
A flowerless prime-tide in these drooping meadows;
To push his beauties forth each primrose pauseth,
Our lilies and our roses like coy widows
    Shut in their buds, their beauties, and bemoan them,
    Because my Phillis doth not smile upon them.

The trees by my redoubled sighs long blasted
Call for thy balm-sweet breath and sunny eyes,
To whom all nature's comforts are hand-fasted;
Breathe, look on them, and they to life arise;
    They have new liveries with each smile thou lendest,
    And droop with me, when thy fair brow thou bendest.

I woo thee, Phillis, with more earnest weeping

Than Niobe for her dead issue spent;
I pray thee, nymph who hast our spring in keeping,
Thou mistress of our flowers and my content,
    Come home, and glad our meads of winter weary,
    And make thy woeful Damon blithe and merry.

Else will I captive all my hopes again,
And shut them up in prisons of despair,
And weep such tears as shall destroy this plain,
And sigh such sighs as shall eclipse the air,
    And cry such cries as love that hears my crying
    Shall faint and weep for grief and fall a-dying.

My little world hath vowed no sun shall glad it,
Except thy little world her light discover,
Of which heavens would grow proud if so they had it.
Oh how I fear lest absent Jove should love her!
    I fear it, Phillis, for he never saw one
    That had more heaven-sweet looks to lure and awe one.

I swear to thee, all-seeing sovereign
Rolling heaven's circles round about our center,
Except my Phillis safe return again,
No joy to heart, no meat to mouth shall enter.
    All hope (but future hope to be renowned,
    For weeping Phillis) shall in tears be drowned.

DEMADES

How large a scope lends Damon to his moan,
Wafting those treasures of his happy wit
In registering his woeful woe-begone!
Ah bend thy muse to matters far more fit!
    For time shall come when Phillis is interred,
    That Damon shall confess that he hath erred.

When nature's riches shall, by time dissolved,
Call thee to see with more judicial eye

How Phillis' beauties are to dust resolved,
Thou then shalt ask thyself the reason why
 Thou wert so fond, since Phillis was so frail,
 To praise her gifts that should so quickly fail.

Have mercy on thyself, cease being idle,
Let reason claim and gain of will his homage;
Rein in these brain-sick thoughts with judgment's bridle,
A short prevention helps a mighty domage.
 If Phillis love, love her, yet love her so
 That if she fly, thou may'st love's fire forego.

Play with the fire, yet die not in the flame;
Show passions in thy words, but not in heart;
Lest when thou think to bring thy thoughts in frame,
Thou prove thyself a prisoner by thine art.
 Play with these babes of love, as apes with glasses,
 And put no trust in feathers, wind, or lasses.

DAMON

Did not thine age yield warrantise, old man,
Impatience would enforce me to offend thee;
Me list not now thy forward skill to scan,
Yet will I pray that love may mend or end thee.
 Spring flowers, sea-tides, earth, grass, sky, stars shall banish,
 Before the thoughts of love or Phillis vanish.

So get thee gone, and fold thy tender sheep,
For lo, the great automaton of day
In Isis stream his golden locks doth steep;
Sad even her dusky mantle doth display;
 Light-flying fowls, the posts of night, disport them,
 And cheerful-looking vesper doth consort them.

Come you, my careful flock, forego you master,
I'll fold you up and after fall a-sighing;
Words have no worth my secret wounds to plaster;

Naught may refresh my joys but Phillis nighing.
    Farewell, old Demades.

DEMADES

                    Damon, farewell.
How 'gainst advice doth headlong youth rebel!

AN ELEGY

Ah cruel winds, why call you hence away?
Why make you breach betwixt my soul and me?
Ye traitorous floods, why nil your floats delay
Until my latest moans discoursèd be?
For though ye salt sea-gods withhold the rain
Of all your floats and gentle winds be still,
While I have wept such tears as might restrain
The rage of tides and winds against their will.
Ah shall I love your sight, bright shining eyes?
And must my soul his life and glory leave?
Must I forsake the bower where solace lives,
To trust to tickle fates that still deceive?
Alas, so wills the wanton queen of change,
That each man tract this labyrinth of life
With slippery steps, now wronged by fortune strange,
Now drawn by counsel from the maze of strife!
Now drawn by counsel from the maze of strife!
Ah joy! No joy because so soon thou fleetest,
Hours, days, and times inconstant in your being!
Oh life! No life, since with such chance thou meetest!
Oh eyes! No eyes, since you must lose your seeing!
Soul, be thou sad, dissolve thy living powers
To crystal tears, and by their pores express
The grief that my distressèd soul devours!
Clothe thou my body all in heaviness;
My suns appeared fair smiling full of pleasure,
But now the vale of absence overclouds them;
They fed my heart with joys exceeding measure
Which now shall die, since absence needs must shroud them.
Yea, die! Oh death, sweet death, vouchsafe that blessing,
That I may die the death whilst she regardeth!
For sweet were death, and sweet were death's oppressing,
If she look on who all my life awardeth.
Oh thou that art the portion of my joy,

Yet not the portion, for thou art the prime;
Suppose my griefs, conceive the deep annoy
That wounds my soul upon this sorry time!
Pale is my face, and in my pale confesses
The pain I suffer, since I needs must leave thee.
Red are mine eyes through tears that them oppresses,
Dulled are my sp'rits since fates do now bereave thee.
And now, ah now, my plaints are quite prevented!
The winds are fair the sails are hoisèd high,
The anchors weighed, and now quite discontented,
Grief so subdues my heart as it should die.
A faint farewell with trembling hand I tender,
And with my tears my papers are distained.
Which closèd up, my heart in them I render,
To tell thee how at parting I complained.
Vouchsafe his message that doth bring farewell,
And for my sake let him with beauty dwell.

THIRSIS EGLOGA SECUNDA

Muses help me, sorrow swarmeth,
Eyes are fraught with seas of languish;
Heavy hope my solace harmeth,
Mind's repast is bitter anguish.

Eye of day regarded never
Certain trust in world untrusty;
Flattering hope beguileth ever
Weary, old, and wanton lusty.

Dawn of day beholds enthronèd
Fortune's darling, proud and dreadless;
Darksome night doth hear him moanèd,
Who before was rich and needless.

Rob the sphere of lines united,
Make a sudden void in nature;
Force the day to be benighted,
Reave the cause of time and creature;

Ere the world will cease to vary,
This I weep for, this I sorrow.
Muses, if you please to tarry,
Further helps I mean to borrow.

Courted once by fortune's favour,
Compassed now with envy's curses,
All my thoughts of sorrow savour,
Hopes run fleeting like the sources.

Ay me! Wanton scorn hath maimèd
All the joy my heart enjoyèd;
Thoughts their thinking have disclaimèd,
Hate my hopes hath quite annoyèd.

Scant regard my weal hath scanted,
Looking coy hath forced my lowering;
Nothing liked where nothing wanted
Weds mine eyes to ceaseless showering.

Former love was once admirèd,
Present favour is estrangèd,
Loath the pleasure long desirèd;
Thus both men and thoughts are changèd.

Lovely swain with lucky guiding,
Once (but now no more so friended)
Thou my flocks hast had in minding,
From the morn till day was ended.

Drink and fodder, food and folding,
Had my lambs and ewes together;
I with them was still beholding,
Both in warmth and winter weather.

Now they languish since refusèd,
Ewes and lambs are pained with pining;
I with ewes and lambs confusèd,
All unto our deaths declining.

Silence, leave thy cave obscurèd;
Deign a doleful swain to tender;
Though disdains I have endurèd,
Yet I am no deep offender.

Phillis' son can with his finger
Hide his scar, it is so little;
Little sin a day to linger,
Wise men wander in a tittle.

Thriftless yet my swain have turnèd,
Though my sun he never showeth:

Though I weep, I am not mournèd;
Though I want, no pity groweth.

Yet for pity love my muses;
Gentle silence be their cover;
They must leave their wonted uses,
Since I leave to be a lover.

They shall live with thee inclosèd,
I will loathe my pen and paper
Art shall never be supposèd,
Sloth shall quench the watching taper.

Kiss them, silence, kiss them kindly
Though I leave them, yet I love them;
Though my wit have led them blindly,
Yet my swain did once approve them.

I will travel soils removèd,
Night and morrow never merry;
Thou shalt harbour that I lovèd,
I will love that makes me weary.

If perchance the sheep estrayeth,
In thy walks and shades unhaunted,
Tell the teen my heart betrayeth,
How neglect my joys hath daunted.

XXI

Ye heralds of my heart, mine ardent groans,
O tears which gladly would burst out to brooks,
Oh spent on fruitless sand my surging moans,
Oh thoughts enthralled unto care-boding looks!
    Ah just laments of my unjust distress,
Ah fond desires whom reason could not guide!
Oh hopes of love that intimate redress,
Yet prove the load-stars unto bad betide!
    When will you cease? Or shall pain never-ceasing,
Seize oh my heart? Oh mollify your rage,
Lest your assaults with over-swift increasing,
Procure my death, or call on timeless age.
    What if they do? They shall but feed the fire,
    Which I have kindled by my fond desire.

XXII

Fair art thou, Phillis, ay, so fair, sweet maid,
As nor the sun, nor I have seen more fair;
For in thy cheeks sweet roses are embayed,
And gold more pure than gold doth gild thy hair.
  Sweet bees have hived their honey on thy tongue,
And Hebe spiced her nectar with thy breath;
About thy neck do all the graces throng,
And lay such baits as might entangle death.
  In such a breast what heart would not be thrall?
From such sweet arms who would not wish embraces?
At thy fair hands who wonders not at all,
Wonder itself through ignorance embases?
  Yet natheless though wondrous gifts you call these,
  My faith is far more wonderful than all these.

XXIII

    Burst, burst, poor heart! Thou hast no longer hope;
Captive mine eyes unto eternal sleep;
Let all my senses have no further scope;
Let death be lord of me and all my sheep!
    For Phillis hath betrothèd fierce disdain,
That makes his mortal mansion in her heart;
And though my tongue have long time taken pain
To sue divorce and wed her to desert,
    She will not yield, my words can have no power;
She scorns my faith, she laughs at my sad lays,
She fills my soul with never ceasing sour,
Who filled the world with volumes of her praise.
        In such extremes what wretch can cease to crave
        His peace from death, who can no mercy have!

XXIV

No glory makes me glorious or glad,
Nor pleasure may to pleasure me dispose,
No comfort can revive my senses sad,
Nor hope enfranchise me with one repose.
    Nor in her absence taste I one delight,
Nor in her presence am I well content;
Was never time gave term to my despite,
Nor joy that dried the tears of my lament.
    Nor hold I hope of weal in memory,
Nor have I thought to change my restless grief,
Nor doth my conquest yield me sovereignty,
Nor hope repose, nor confidence relief.
    For why? She sorts her frowns and favours so,
    As when I gain or lose I cannot know.

XXV

  I wage the combat with two mighty foes,
Which are more strong than I ten thousand fold;
The one is when thy pleasure I do lose,
The other, when thy person I behold.
  In seeing thee a swarm of loves confound me,
And cause my death in spite of my resist,
And if I see thee not, thy want doth wound me,
For in thy sight my comfort doth consist.
  The one in me continual care createth,
The other doth occasion my desire;
The one the edge of all my joy rebateth,
The other makes me a phœnix in love's fire.
   So that I grieve when I enjoy your presence,
   And die for grief by reason of your absence.

XXVI

I'll teach thee, lovely Phillis, what love is.
It is a vision seeming such as thou,
That flies as fast as it assaults mine eyes;
It is affection that doth reason miss;
It is a shape of pleasure like to you,
Which meets the eye, and seen on sudden dies;
It is a doubled grief, a spark of pleasure
Begot by vain desire. And this is love,
Whom in our youth we count our chiefest treasure,
In age for want of power we do reprove.
Yea, such a power is love, whose loss is pain,
And having got him we repent our gain.

XXVII

Fair eyes, whilst fearful I your fair admire,
By unexpressèd sweetness that I gain,
My memory of sorrow doth expire,
And falcon-like, I tower joy's heavens amain.
But when your suns in oceans of their glory
Shut up their day-bright shine, I die for thought;
So pass my joys as doth a new-played story,
And one poor sigh breathes all delight to naught.
So to myself I live not, but for you;
For you I live, and you I love, but none else,
Oh then, fair eyes, whose light I live to view,
Or poor forlorn despised to live alone else,
Look sweet, since from the pith of contemplation
Love gathereth life, and living, breedeth passion.

XXVIII

Not causeless were you christened, gentle flowers,
The one of faith, the other fancy's pride;
For she who guides both faith and fancy's power,
In your fair colors wraps her ivory side.
    As one of you hath whiteness without stain,
So spotless is my love and never tainted;
And as the other shadoweth faith again,
Such is my lass, with no fond change acquainted.
    And as nor tyrant sun nor winter weather
May ever change sweet amaranthus' hue,
So she though love and fortune join together,
Will never leave to be both fair and true.
    And should I leave thee then, thou pretty elf?
    Nay, first let Damon quite forget himself.

XXIX

I feel myself endangered beyond reason,
My death already 'twixt the cup and lip,
Because my proud desire through cursèd treason,
Would make my hopes mount heaven, which cannot skip;
    My fancy still requireth at my hands
Such things as are not, cannot, may not be,
And my desire although my power withstands,
Will give me wings, who never yet could flee.
    What then remains except my maimèd soul
Extort compassion from love-flying age,
Or if naught else their fury may control,
To call on death that quells affection's rage;
Which death shall dwell with me and never fly,
    Which death shall dwell with me and never fly,
    Since vain desire seeks that hope doth deny.

XXX

    I do compare unto thy youthly clear,
Which always bides within thy flow'ring prime,
The month of April, that bedews our clime
With pleasant flowers, when as his showers appear.
    Before thy face shall fly false cruelty,
Before his face the doly season fleets;
Mild been his looks, thine eyes are full of sweets;
Firm is his course, firm is thy loyalty.
    He paints the fields through liquid crystal showers,
Thou paint'st my verse with Pallas, learnèd flowers;
With Zephirus' sweet, breath he fills the plains,
And thou my heart with weeping sighs dost wring;
     His brows are dewed with morning's crystal spring,
     Thou mak'st my eyes with tears bemoan my pains.

XXXI

    Devoid of reason, thrall to foolish ire,
I walk and chase a savage fairy still,
Now near the flood, straight on the mounting hill,
Now midst the woods of youth, and vain desire.
    For leash I bear a cord of careful grief;
For brach I lead an over-forward mind;
My hounds are thoughts, and rage despairing blind,
Pain, cruelty, and care without relief.
    But they perceiving that my swift pursuit
My flying fairy cannot overtake,
With open mouths their prey on me do make,
Like hungry hounds that lately lost their suit.
    And full of fury on their master feed,
    To hasten on my hapless death with speed.

XXXII

A thousand times to think and think the same,
To two fair eyes to show a naked heart,
Great thirst with bitter liquor to restrain,
To take repast of care and crooked smart;
　　To sigh full oft without relent of ire,
To die for grief and yet conceal the tale,
To others' will to fashion my desire,
To pine in looks disguised through pensive-pale;
　　A short dispite, a faith unfeignèd true,
To love my foe, and set my life at naught,
With heedless eyes mine endless harms to view,
A will to speak, a fear to tell the thought;
　　To hope for all, yet for despair to die,
　　Is of my life the certain destiny.

XXXIII

When first sweet Phillis, whom I must adore,
Gan with her beauties bless our wond'ring sky,
The son of Rhea, from their fatal store
Made all the gods to grace her majesty.
    Apollo first his golden rays among,
Did form the beauty of her bounteous eyes;
He graced her with his sweet melodious song,
And made her subject of his poesies.
    The warrior Mars bequeathed her fierce disdain,
Venus her smile, and Phœbe all her fair,
Python his voice, and Ceres all her grain,
The morn her locks and fingers did repair.
    Young Love, his bow, and Thetis gave her feet;
    Clio her praise, Pallas her science sweet.

XXXIV

     I would in rich and golden-coloured rain,
With tempting showers in pleasant sort descend
Into fair Phillis' lap, my lovely friend,
When sleep her sense with slumber doth restrain.
     I would be changèd to a milk-white bull,
When midst the gladsome fields she should appear,
By pleasant fineness to surprise my dear,
Whilst from their stalks, she pleasant flowers did pull.
     I were content to weary out my pain,
To be Narsissus so she were a spring,
To drown in her those woes my heart do wring.
And more; I wish transformèd to remain,
       That whilst I thus in pleasure's lap did lie,
       I might refresh desire, which else would die.

XXXV

I hope and fear, I pray and hold my peace,
Now freeze my thoughts and straight they fry again,
I now admire and straight my wonders cease,
I loose my bonds and yet myself restrain;
    This likes me most that leaves me discontent,
My courage serves and yet my heart doth fail,
My will doth climb whereas my hopes are spent,
I laugh at love, yet when he comes I quail;
    The more I strive, the duller bide I still.
I would be thralled, and yet I freedom love,
I would redress, yet hourly feed mine ill,
I would repine, and dare not once reprove;
    And for my love I am bereft of power,
    And strengthless strive my weakness to devour.

XXXVI

    If so I seek the shades, I presently do see
The god of love forsakes his bow and sit me by;
If that I think to write, his Muses pliant be
If so I plain my grief, the wanton boy will cry,
    If I lament his pride, he doth increase my pain;
If tears my cheeks attaint, his cheeks are moist with moan;
If I disclose the wounds the which my heart hath slain,
He takes his fascia off, and wipes them dry anon.
If so I walk the woods, the woods are his delight;
    If I myself torment, he bathes him in my blood;
He will my soldier be if once I wend to fight,
If seas delight, he steers my bark amidst the hood.
    In brief, the cruel god doth never from me go,
    But makes my lasting love eternal with my woe.

XXXVII

These fierce incessant waves that stream along my face,
Which show the certain proof of my ne'er-ceasing pains,
Fair Phillis, are no tears that trickle from my brains;
For why? Such streams of ruth within me find no place.
    These floods that wet my cheeks are gathered from thy grace
And thy perfections, and from hundred thousand flowers
Which from thy beauties spring; whereto I medley showers
Of rose and lilies too, the colours of thy face.
    My love doth serve for fire, my heart the furnace is,
The aperries of my sighs augment the burning flame,
The limbec is mine eye that doth distil the same;
And by how much my fire is violent and sly,
      By so much doth it cause the waters mount on high,
      That shower from out mine eyes, for to assuage my miss.

XXXVIII

Who lives enthralled to Cupid and his flame,
From day to day is changed in sundry sort;
The proof whereof myself may well report,
Who oft transformed by him may teach the same.
    I first was turned into a wounded hart,
That bare the bloody arrow in my side;
Then to a swan that midst the waters glide,
With piteous voice presaged my deadly smart;
    Eftsoons I waxed a faint and fading flower;
Then was I made a fountain sudden dry,
Distilling all my tears from troubled eye;
Now am I salamander by his power,
    Living in flames, but hope ere long to be
    A voice, to talk my mistress' majesty.

XXXIX

    My matchless mistress, whose delicious eyes
Have power to perfect nature's privy wants,
Even when the sun in greatest pomp did rise,
With pretty tread did press the tender plants.
      Each stalk whilst forth she stalks, to kiss her feet
      Is proud with pomp, and prodigal of sweet.
Her fingers fair in favouring every flower
That wooed their ivory for a wishèd touch,
By chance – sweet chance! – upon a blessed hour
Did pluck the flower where Love himself did couch.
      Where Love did couch by summer toil suppressed,
      And sought his sleeps within so sweet a nest.
The virgin's hand that held the wanton thrall,
Imprisoned him within the roseate leaves;
And twixt her teats, with favour did install
The lovely rose, where Love his rest receives.
      The lad that felt the soft and sweet so nigh,
      Drowned in delights, disdains his liberty;
And said, let Venus seek another son,
For here my only matchless mother is;
From whose fair orient orbs the drink doth run,
That deifies my state with greater bliss.
      This said, he sucked, my mistress blushing smiled,
      Since Love was both her prisoner and her child.

AN ODE

Now I find thy looks were feignèd,
Quickly lost, and quickly gainèd;
Soft thy skin, like wool of wethers,
Heart unstable, light as feathers,
Tongue untrusty, subtile-sighted,
Wanton will, with change delighted,
Siren pleasant, foe to reason,
Cupid plague thee for this treason!

Of thine eyes, I made my mirror,
From thy beauty came mine error,
All thy words I counted witty,
All thy smiles I deemèd pity.
Thy false tears that me aggrievèd,
First of all my trust deceivèd.
Siren pleasant, foe to reason,
Cupid plague thee for this treason!

Feigned acceptance when I askèd,
Lovely words with cunning maskèd,
Holy vows but heart unholy;
Wretched man, my trust was folly!
Lily white and pretty winking,
Solemn vows, but sorry thinking.
Siren pleasant, foe to reason,
Cupid plague thee for this treason!

Now I see, O seemly cruel,
Others warm them at my fuel!
Wit shall guide me in this durance,
Since in love is no assurance.
Change thy pasture, take thy pleasure;
Beauty is a fading treasure.
Siren pleasant, foe to reason,

Cupid plague thee for this treason!

Prime youth lusts not age still follow,
And make white these tresses yellow;
Wrinkled face for looks delightful
Shall acquaint the dame despightful;
And when time shall eat thy glory,
Then too late thou wilt be sorry.
Siren pleasant, foe to reason,
Cupid plague thee for thy treason!

XL

Resembling none, and none so poor as I,
Poor to the world, and poor in each esteem,
Whose first-born loves at first obscured did die,
And bred no fame but flame of base misdeem,
　　Under the ensign of whose tirèd pen,
Love's legions forth have masked, by others masked;
Think how I live wrongèd by ill-tongued men,
Not master of myself, to all wrongs tasked!
　　Oh thou that canst, and she that may do all things,
Support these languishing conceits that perish!
Look on their growth; perhaps these silly small things
May win this wordly palm, so you do cherish.
　　Homer hath vowed, and I with him do vow this,
　　He will and shall revive, if you allow this.

CHLORIS

OR, THE COMPLAINT OF THE PASSIONATE
DESPISED SHEPHERD

BY

WILLIAM SMITH

(1596)

TO THE MOST EXCELLENT AND LEARNED SHEPHERD
COLIN CLOUT

I

Colin my dear and most entire beloved,
My muse audacious stoops her pitch to thee,
Desiring that thy patience be not moved
By these rude lines, written here you see;
Fain would my muse whom cruel love hath wronged,
Shroud her love labours under thy protection,
And I myself with ardent zeal have longed
That thou mightst know to thee my true affection.
Therefore, good Colin, graciously accept
A few sad sonnets which my muse hath framed;
Though they but newly from the shell are crept,
Suffer them not by envy to be blamed,
But underneath the shadow of thy wings
Give warmth to these young-hatchèd orphan things.

II

Give warmth to these young-hatchèd orphan things,
Which chill with cold to thee for succour creep;
They of my study are the budding springs;
Longer I cannot them in silence keep.
They will be gadding sore against my mind.
But courteous shepherd, if they run astray,
Conduct them that they may the pathway find,
And teach them how the mean observe they may.
Thou shalt them ken by their discording notes,
Their weeds are plain, such as poor shepherds wear;
Unshapen, torn, and ragged are their coats,
Yet forth they wand'ring are devoid of fear.
    They which have tasted of the muses' spring,
    I hope will smile upon the tunes they sing.

TO ALL SHEPHERDS IN GENERAL

You whom the world admires for rarest style,
You which have sung the sonnets of true love,
Upon my maiden verse with favour smile,
Whose weak-penned muse to fly too soon doth prove;
Before her feathers have their full perfection,
She soars aloft, pricked on by blind affection.

You whose deep wits, ingine, and industry,
The everlasting palm of praise have won,
You paragons of learnèd poesy,
Favour these mists, which fall before your sun,
Intentions leading to a more effect
If you them grace but with your mild aspect.

And thou the Genius of my ill-tuned note,
Whose beauty urgèd hath my rustic vein
Through mighty oceans of despair to float,
That I in rime thy cruelty complain:
Vouchsafe to read these lines both harsh and bad
Nuntiates of woe with sorrow being clad.

CHLORIS

I

Courteous Calliope, vouchsafe to lend
Thy helping hand to my untunèd song,
And grace these lines which I to write pretend,
Compelled by love which doth poor Corin wrong.
And those thy sacred sisters I beseech,
Which on Parnassus' mount do ever dwell,
To shield my country muse and rural speech
By their divine authority and spell.
Lastly to thee, O Pan, the shepherds' king,
And you swift-footed Dryades I call;
Attend to hear a swain in verse to sing
Sonnets of her that keeps his heart in thrall!
    O Chloris, weigh the task I undertake!
    Thy beauty subject of my song I make.

II

Thy beauty subject of my song I make,
O fairest fair, on whom depends my life!
Refuse not then the task I undertake,
To please thy rage and to appease my strife;
But with one smile remunerate my toil,
None other guerdon I of thee desire.
Give not my lowly muse new-hatched the foil,
But warmth that she may at the length aspire
Unto the temples of thy star-bright eyes,
Upon whose round orbs perfect beauty sits,
From whence such glorious crystal beams arise,
As best my Chloris' seemly face befits;
    Which eyes, which beauty, which bright crystal beam,
    Which face of thine hath made my love extreme.

III

Feed, silly sheep, although your keeper pineth,
Yet like to Tantalus doth see his food.
Skip you and leap, no bright Apollo shineth,
Whilst I bewail my sorrows in yon wood,
Where woeful Philomela doth record,
And sings with notes of sad and dire lament
The tragedy wrought by her sisters' lord;
I'll bear a part in her black discontent.
That pipe which erst was wont to make you glee
Upon these downs whereon you careless graze,
Shall to her mournful music tunèd be.
Let not my plaints, poor lambkins, you amaze;
    There underneath that dark and dusky bower,
    Whole showers of tears to Chloris I will pour.

IV

Whole showers of tears to Chloris I will pour,
As true oblations of my sincere love,
If that will not suffice, most fairest flower,
Then shall my sighs thee unto pity move.
If neither tears nor sighs can aught prevail,
My streaming blood thine anger shall appease,
This hand of mine by vigour shall assail
To tear my heart asunder thee to please.
Celestial powers on you I invocate;
You know the chaste affections of my mind,
I never did my faith yet violate;
Why should my Chloris then be so unkind?
    That neither tears, nor sighs, nor streaming blood,
    Can unto mercy move her cruel mood.

V

You fawns and silvans, when my Chloris brings
Her flocks to water in your pleasant plains,
Solicit her to pity Corin's strings,
The smart whereof for her he still sustains.
For she is ruthless of my woeful song;
My oaten reed she not delights to hear.
O Chloris, Chloris! Corin thou dost wrong,
Who loves thee better than his own heart dear.
The flames of Aetna are not half so hot
As is the fire which thy disdain hath bread.
Ah cruel fates, why do you then besot
Poor Corin's soul with love, when love is fled?
    Either cause cruel Chloris to relent,
    Or let me die upon the wound she sent!

VI

You lofty pines, co-partners of my woe,
When Chloris sitteth underneath your shade,
To her those sighs and tears I pray you show,
Whilst you attending I for her have made.
Whilst you attending, droppèd have sweet balm
In token that you pity my distress,
Zephirus hath your stately boughs made calm.
Whilst I to you my sorrows did express,
The neighbour mountains bended have their tops,
When they have heard my rueful melody,
And elves in rings about me leaps and hops,
To frame my passions to their jollity.
    Resounding echoes from their obscure caves,
    Reiterate what most my fancy craves.

VII

What need I mourn, seeing Pan our sacred king
Was of that nymph fair Syrinx coy disdained?
The world's great light which comforteth each thing,
All comfortless for Daphne's sake remained.
If gods can find no help to heal the sore
Made by love's shafts, which pointed are with fire,
Unhappy Corin, then thy chance deplore,
Sith they despair by wanting their desire.
I am not Pan though I a shepherd be,
Yet is my love as fair as Syrinx was.
My songs cannot with Phœbus' tunes agree,
Yet Chloris' doth his Daphne's far surpass.
    How much more fair by so much more unkind,
    Than Syrinx coy, or Daphne, I her find!

VIII

No sooner had fair Phœbus trimmed his car,
Being newly risen from Aurora's bed,
But I in whom despair and hope did war,
My unpenned flock unto the mountains led.
Tripping upon the snow-soft downs I spied
Three nymphs more fairer than those beautys three
Which did appear to Paris on mount Ide.
Coming more near, my goddess I there see;
For she the field-nymphs oftentimes doth haunt,
To hunt with them the fierce and savage boar;
And having sported virelays they chaunt,
Whilst I unhappy helpless cares deplore.
    There did I call to her, ah too unkind!
    But tiger-like, of me she had no mind.

IX

Unto the fountain where fair Delia chaste
The proud Acteon turnèd to a hart,
I drove my flock, that water sweet to taste,
'Cause from the welkin Phœbus 'gan depart.
There did I see the nymph whom I admire,
Rememb'ring her locks, of which the yellow hue
Made blush the beauties of her curlèd wire,
Which Jove himself with wonder well might view;
Then red with ire, her tresses she berent,
And weeping hid the beauty of her face,
Whilst I amazèd at her discontent,
With tears and sighs do humbly sue for grace;
    But she regarding neither tears nor moan,
    Flies from the fountain leaving me alone.

X

Am I a Gorgon that she doth me fly,
Or was I hatchèd in the river Nile?
Or doth my Chloris stand in doubt that I
With syren songs do seek her to beguile?
If any one of these she can object
'Gainst me, which chaste affected love protest,
Then might my fortunes by her frowns be checked,
And blameless she from scandal free might rest.
But seeing I am no hideous monster born,
But have that shape which other men do bear,
Which form great Jupiter did never scorn,
Amongst his subjects here on earth to wear,
    Why should she then that soul with sorrow fill,
    Which vowèd hath to love and serve her still?

XI

Tell me, my dear, what moves thy ruthless mind
To be so cruel, seeing thou art so fair?
Did nature frame thy beauty so unkind?
Or dost thou scorn to pity my despair?
O no, it was not nature's ornament,
But wingèd love's unpartial cruel wound,
Which in my heart is ever permanent,
Until my Chloris make me whole and sound.
O glorious love-god, think on my heart's grief;
Let not thy vassal pine through deep disdain;
By wounding Chloris I shall find relief,
If thou impart to her some of my pain.
    She doth thy temples and thy shrines abject;
    They with Amintas' flowers by me are decked.

XII

Cease, eyes, to weep sith none bemoans your weeping;
Leave off, good muse, to sound the cruel name
Of my love's queen which hath my heart in keeping,
Yet of my love doth make a jesting game!
Long hath my sufferance laboured to inforce
One pearl of pity from her pretty eyes,
Whilst I with restless oceans of remorse
Bedew the banks where my fair Chloris lies,
Where my fair Chloris bathes her tender skin,
And doth triumph to see such rivers fall
From those moist springs, which never dry have been
Since she their honour hath detained in thrall;
>   And still she scorns one favouring smile to show
>   Unto those waves proceeding from my woe.

XIII

A Dream

What time fair Titan in the zenith sat,
And equally the fixèd poles did heat,
When to my flock my daily woes I chat,
And underneath a broad beech took my seat,
The dreaming god which Morpheus poets call,
Augmenting fuel to my Aetna's fire,
With sleep possessing my weak senses all,
In apparitions makes my hopes aspire.
Methought I saw the nymph I would imbrace,
With arms abroad coming to me for help,
A lust-led satyr having her in chase
Which after her about the fields did yelp.
I seeing my love in perplexèd plight,
A sturdy bat from off an oak I reft,
And with the ravisher continue fight
Till breathless I upon the earth him left.
Then when my coy nymph saw her breathless foe,
With kisses kind she gratifies my pain,
Protesting never rigour more to show.
Happy was I this good hap to obtain;
But drowsy slumbers flying to their cell,
My sudden joy converted was to bale;
My wonted sorrows still with me do dwell.
I lookèd round about on hill and dale,
    But I could neither my fair Chloris view,
    Nor yet the satyr which erstwhile I slew.

XIV

Mournful Amintas, thou didst pine with care,
Because the fates by their untimely doom
Of life bereft thy loving Phillis fair,
When thy love's spring did first begin to bloom.
My care doth countervail that care of thine,
And yet my Chloris draws her angry breath;
My hopes still hoping hopeless now repine,
For living she doth add to me but death.
Thy Phinis, dying, lovèd thee full dear;
My Chloris, living, hates poor Corin's love,
Thus doth my woe as great as thine appear,
Though sundry accents both our sorrows move.
  Thy swan-like songs did show thy dying anguish;
  These weeping truce-men show I living languish.

XV

These weeping truce-men show I living languish,
My woeful wailings tells my discontent;
Yet Chloris nought esteemeth of mine anguish,
My thrilling throbs her heart cannot relent.
My kids to hear the rimes and roundelays
Which I on wasteful hills was wont to sing,
Did more delight the lark in summer days,
Whose echo made the neighbour groves to ring.
But now my flock all drooping bleats and cries,
Because my pipe, the author of their sport,
All rent and torn and unrespected lies;
Their lamentations do my cares consort.
    They cease to feed and listen to the plaint
    Which I pour forth unto a cruel saint.

XVI

Which I pour forth unto a cruel saint,
Who merciless my prayers doth attend,
Who tiger-like doth pity my complaint,
And never ear unto my woes will lend!
But still false hope dispairing life deludes,
And tells my fancy I shall grace obtain;
But Chloris fair my orisons concludes
With fearful frowns, presagers of my pain.
Thus do I spend the weary wand'ring day,
Oppressèd with a chaos of heart's grief;
Thus I consume the obscure night away,
Neglecting sleep which brings all cares relief;
  Thus do I pass my ling'ring life in woe;
  But when my bliss will come I do not know.

XVII

The perils which Leander took in hand
Fair Hero's love and favour to obtain,
When void of fear securely leaving land,
Through Hellespont he swam to Cestos' main,
His dangers should not counterpoise my toil,
If my dear love would once but pity show,
To quench these flames which in my breast do broil,
Or dry these springs which from mine eyes do flow.
Not only Hellespont but ocean seas,
For her sweet sake to ford I would attempt,
So that my travels would her ire appease,
My soul from thrall and languish to exempt.
    O what is't not poor I would undertake,
    If labour could my peace with Chloris make!

XVIII

My love, I cannot thy rare beauties place
Under those forms which many writers use:
Some like to stones compare their mistress' face;
Some in the name of flowers do love abuse;
Some makes their love a goldsmith's shop to be,
Where orient pearls and precious stones abound;
In my conceit these far do disagree
The perfect praise of beauty forth to sound.
O Chloris, thou dost imitate thyself,
Self's imitating passeth precious stones,
Or all the eastern Indian golden pelf;
Thy red and white with purest fair atones;
     Matchless for beauty nature hath thee framed,
     Only unkind and cruel thou art named!

XIX

The hound by eating grass doth find relief,
For being sick it is his choicest meat;
The wounded hart doth ease his pain and grief
If he the herb dictamion may eat;
The loathsome snake renews his sight again,
When he casts off his withered coat and hue;
The sky-bred eagle fresh age doth obtain
When he his beak decayed doth renew.
I worse than these whose sore no salve can cure,
Whose grief no herb nor plant nor tree can ease;
Remediless, I still must pain endure,
Till I my Chloris' furious mood can please;
    She like the scorpion gave to me a wound,
    And like the scorpion she must make me sound.

XX

Ye wasteful woods, bear witness of my woe,
Wherein my plaints did oftentimes abound;
Ye careless birds my sorrows well do know,
They in your songs were wont to make a sound!
Thou pleasant spring canst record likewise bear
Of my designs and sad disparagement,
When thy transparent billows mingled were
With those downfalls which from mine eyes were sent!
The echo of my still-lamenting cries,
From hollow vaults in treble voice resoundeth,
And then into the empty air it flies,
And back again from whence it came reboundeth.
 That nymph unto my clamors doth reply,
 Being likewise scorned in love as well as I.

XXI

Being likewise scorned in love as well as I
By that self-loving boy, which did disdain
To hear her after him for love to cry,
For which in dens obscure she doth remain;
Yet doth she answer to each speech and voice,
And renders back the last of what we speak,
But specially, if she might have her choice,
She of unkindness would her talk forth break.
She loves to hear of love's most sacred name,
Although, poor nymph, in love she was despised;
And ever since she hides her head for shame,
That her true meaning was so lightly prised;
  She pitying me, part of my woes doth bear,
  As you, good shepherds, listening now shall hear.

XXII

O fairest fair, to thee I make my plaint,
                              (my plaint)
To thee from whom my cause of grief doth spring;
                              (doth spring)
Attentive be unto the groans, sweet saint,
                              (sweet saint)
Which unto thee in doleful tunes I sing.
                              (I sing)
My mournful muse doth always speak of thee;
                              (of thee)
My love is pure, O do it not disdain!
                              (disdain)
With bitter sorrow still oppress not me,
                              (not me)
But mildly look upon me which complain.
                              (which complain)
Kill not my true-affecting thoughts, but give
                              (but give)
Such precious balm of comfort to my heart,
                              (my heart)
That casting off despair in hope to live,
                              (hope to live)
I may find help at length to ease my smart.
                              (to ease my smart)
So shall you add such courage to my love,
                              (my love)
That fortune false my faith shall not remove.
                              (shall not remove)

XXIII

The phœnix fair which rich Arabia breeds,
When wasting time expires her tragedy,
No more on Phœbus' radiant rays she feeds,
But heapeth up great store of spicery;
And on a lofty towering cedar tree,
With heavenly substance she herself consumes,
From whence she young again appears to be,
Out of the cinders of her peerless plumes.
So I which long have frièd in love's flame,
The fire not made of spice but sighs and tears,
Revive again in hope disdain to shame,
And put to flight the author of my fears.
    Her eyes revive decaying life in me,
    Though they augmenters of my thraldom be.

XXIV

Though they augmenters of my thraldom be,
For her I live and her I love and none else;
O then, fair eyes, look mildly upon me,
Who poor, despised, forlorn must live alone else,
And like Amintas haunt the desert cells,
And moanless there breathe out thy cruelty,
Where none but care and melancholy dwells.
I for revenge to Nemesis will cry;
If that will not prevail, my wandering ghost,
Which breathless here this love-scorched trunk shall leave,
Shall unto thee with tragic tidings post,
How thy disdain did life from soul bereave.
    Then all too late my death thou wilt repent,
    When murther's guilt thy conscience shall torment.

XXV

Who doth not know that love is triumphant,
Sitting upon the throne of majesty?
The gods themselves his cruel darts do daunt,
And he, blind boy, smiles at their misery.
Love made great Jove ofttimes transform his shape;
Love made the fierce Alcides stoop at last;
Achilles, stout and bold, could not escape
The direful doom which love upon him cast;
Love made Leander pass the dreadful flood
Which Cestos from Abydos doth divide;
Love made a chaos where proud Ilion stood,
Through love the Carthaginian Dido died.
    Thus may we see how love doth rule and reigns,
    Bringing those under which his power disdains.

XXVI

Though you be fair and beautiful withal,
And I am black for which you me despise,
Know that your beauty subject is to fall,
Though you esteem it at so high a price.
And time may come when that whereof you boast,
Which is your youth's chief wealth and ornament,
Shall withered be by winter's raging frost,
When beauty's pride and flowering years are spent.
Then wilt thou mourn when none shall thee respect;
Then wilt thou think how thou hast scorned my tears;
Then pitiless each one will thee neglect,
When hoary grey shall dye thy yellow hairs;
    Then wilt thou think upon poor Corin's case,
    Who loved thee dear, yet lived in thy disgrace.

XXVII

O Love, leave off with sorrow to torment me;
Let my heart's grief and pining pain content thee!
The breach is made, I give thee leave to enter;
Thee to resist, great god, I dare not venter!
Restless desire doth aggravate mine anguish,
Careful conceits do fill my soul with languish.
Be not too cruel in thy conquest gained,
Thy deadly shafts hath victory obtained;
Batter no more my fort with fierce affection,
But shield me captive under thy protection.
    I yield to thee, O Love, thou art the stronger,
    Raise then thy siege and trouble me no longer!

XXVIII

What cruel star or fate had domination
When I was born, that thus my love is crossed?
Or from what planet had I derivation
That thus my life in seas of woe is crossed?
Doth any live that ever had such hap
That all their actions are of none effect,
Whom fortune never dandled in her lap
But as an abject still doth me reject?
Ah tickle dame! and yet thou constant art
My daily grief and anguish to increase,
And to augment the troubles of my heart
Thou of these bonds wilt never me release;
    So that thy darlings me to be may know
    The true idea of all worldly woe.

XXIX

Some in their hearts their mistress' colours bears;
Some hath her gloves, some other hath her garters,
Some in a bracelet wears her golden hairs,
And some with kisses seal their loving charters.
But I which never favour reapèd yet,
Nor had one pleasant look from her fair brow,
Content myself in silent shade to sit
In hope at length my cares to overplow.
Meanwhile mine eyes shall feed on her fair face,
My sighs shall tell to her my sad designs,
My painful pen shall ever sue for grace
To help my heart, which languishing now pines;
    And I will triumph still amidst my woe
    Till mercy shall my sorrows overflow.

XXX

The raging sea within his limits lies
And with an ebb his flowing doth discharge;
The rivers when beyond their bounds they rise,
Themselves do empty in the ocean large;
But my love's sea which never limit keepeth,
Which never ebbs but always ever floweth,
In liquid salt unto my Chloris weepeth,
Yet frustrate are the tears which he bestoweth.
This sea which first was but a little spring
Is now so great and far beyond all reason,
That it a deluge to my thoughts doth bring,
Which overwhelmed hath my joying season.
    So hard and dry is my saint's cruel mind,
    These waves no way in her to sink can find.

XXXI

These waves no way in her to sink can find
To penetrate the pith of contemplation;
These tears cannot dissolve her hardened mind,
Nor move her heart on me to take compassion;
O then, poor Corin, scorned and quite despised,
Loathe now to live since life procures thy woe;
Enough, thou hast thy heart anatomised,
For her sweet sake which will no pity show;
But as cold winter's storms and nipping frost
Can never change sweet Aramanthus' hue,
So though my love and life by her are crossed.
My heart shall still be constant firm and true.
    Although Erynnis hinders Hymen's rites,
    My fixèd faith against oblivion fights.

XXXII

My fixèd faith against oblivion fights,
And I cannot forget her, pretty elf,
Although she cruel be unto my plights;
Yet let me rather clean forget myself,
Then her sweet name out of my mind should go,
Which is th' elixir of my pining soul,
From whence the essence of my life doth flow,
Whose beauty rare my senses all control;
Themselves most happy evermore accounting,
That such a nymph is queen of their affection,
With ravished rage they to the skies are mounting,
Esteeming not their thraldom nor subjection;
    But still do joy amidst their misery,
    With patience bearing love's captivity.

XXXIII

With patience bearing love's captivity,
Themselves unguilty of his wrath alleging;
These homely lines, abjects of poesy,
For liberty and for their ransom pledging,
And being free they solemnly do vow,
Under his banner ever arms to bear
Against those rebels which do disallow
That love of bliss should be the sovereign heir;
And Chloris if these weeping truce-men may
One spark of pity from thine eyes obtain,
In recompense of their sad heavy lay,
Poor Corin shall thy faithful friend remain;
　　And what I say I ever will approve,
　　No joy may be comparèd to thy love!

XXXIV

The bird of Thrace which doth bewail her rape,
And murthered Itys eaten by his sire,
When she her woes in doleful tunes doth shape,
She sets her breast against a thorny briar;
Because care-charmer sleep should not disturb
The tragic tale which to the night she tells,
She doth her rest and quietness thus curb
Amongst the groves where secret silence dwells:
Even so I wake, and waking wail all night;
Chloris' unkindness slumbers doth expel;
I need not thorn's sweet sleep to put to flight,
Her cruelty my golden rest doth quell,
    That day and night to me are always one,
    Consumed in woe, in tears, in sighs and moan.

XXXV

Like to the shipman in his brittle boat.
Tossèd aloft by the unconstant wind,
By dangerous rocks and whirling gulfs doth float,
Hoping at length the wishèd port to find;
So doth my love in stormy billows sail,
And passeth the gaping Scilla's waves,
In hope at length with Chloris to prevail
And win that prize which most my fancy craves,
Which unto me of value will be more
Then was that rich and wealthy golden fleece.
Which Jason stout from Colchos' island bore
With wind in sails unto the shore of Greece.
    More rich, more rare, more worth her love I prize
    Then all the wealth which under heaven lies.

XXXVI

O what a wound and what a deadly stroke,
Doth Cupid give to us perplexèd lovers,
Which cleaves more fast then ivy doth to oak,
Unto our hearts where he his might discovers!
Though warlike Mars were armèd at all points,
With that tried coat which fiery Vulcan made,
Love's shafts did penetrate his steelèd joints,
And in his breast in streaming gore did wade.
So pitiless is this fell conqueror
That in his mother's paps his arrows stuck;
Such is his rage that he doth not defer
To wound those orbs from whence he life did suck.
  Then sith no mercy he shows to his mother,
  We meekly must his force and rigour smother.

XXXVII

Each beast in field doth wish the morning light;
The birds to Hesper pleasant lays do sing;
The wanton kids well-fed rejoice in night,
Being likewise glad when day begins to spring.
But night nor day are welcome unto me,
Both can bear witness of my lamentation;
All day sad sighing Corin you shall see,
All night he spends in tears and exclamation.
Thus still I live although I take no rest,
But living look as one that is a-dying;
Thus my sad soul with care and grief oppressed,
Seems as a ghost to Styx and Lethe flying.
  Thus hath fond love bereft my youthful years
  Of all good hap before old age appears.

XXXVIII

That day wherein mine eyes cannot her see,
Which is the essence of their crystal sight,
Both blind, obscure and dim that day they be,
And are debarrèd of fair heaven's light;
That day wherein mine ears do want to hear her,
Hearing that day is from me quite bereft;
That day wherein to touch I come not near her,
That day no sense of touching I have left;
That day wherein I lack the fragrant smell,
Which from her pleasant amber breath proceedeth,
Smelling that day disdains with me to dwell,
Only weak hope my pining carcase feedeth.
    But burst, poor heart, thou hast no better hope,
    Since all thy senses have no further scope!

XXXIX

The stately lion and the furious bear
The skill of man doth alter from their kind;
For where before they wild and savage were,
By art both tame and meek you shall them find.
The elephant although a mighty beast,
A man may rule according to his skill;
The lusty horse obeyeth our behest,
For with the curb you may him guide at will.
Although the flint most hard contains the fire,
By force we do his virtue soon obtain,
For with a steel you shall have your desire,
Thus man may all things by industry gain;
  Only a woman if she list not love,
  No art, nor force, can unto pity move.

XL

No art nor force can unto pity move
Her stony heart that makes my heart to pant;
No pleading passions of my extreme love
Can mollify her mind of adamant.
Ah cruel sex, and foe to all mankind,
Either you love or else you hate too much!
A glist'ring show of gold in you we find,
And yet you prove but copper in the touch.
But why, O why, do I so far digress?
Nature you made of pure and fairest mould,
The pomp and glory of man to depress,
And as your slaves in thraldom them to hold;
    Which by experience now too well I prove,
    There is no pain unto the pains of love.

XLI

Fair shepherdess, when as these rustic lines
Comes to thy sight, weigh but with what affection
Thy servile doth depaint his sad designs,
Which to redress of thee he makes election.
If so you scorn, you kill; if you seem coy,
You wound poor Corin to the very heart;
If that you smile, you shall increase his joy;
If these you like, you banish do all smart.
And this I do protest, most fairest fair,
My muse shall never cease that hill to climb,
To which the learnèd Muses do repair,
And all to deify thy name in rime;
    And never none shall write with truer mind,
    As by all proof and trial you shall find.

XLII

Die, die, my hopes! for you do but augment
The burning accents of my deep despair;
Disdain and scorn your downfall do consent;
Tell to the world she is unkind yet fair!
O eyes, close up those ever-running fountains,
For pitiless are all the tears you shed
Wherewith you watered have both dales and mountains!
I see, I see, remorse from her is fled.
Pack hence, ye sighs, into the empty air,
Into the air that none your sound may hear,
Sith cruel Chloris hath of you no care,
Although she once esteemèd you full dear!
    Let sable night all your disgraces cover,
    Yet truer sighs were never sighed by lover.

XLIII

Thou glorious sun, from whence my lesser light
The substance of his crystal shine doth borrow,
Let these my moans find favour in thy sight.
And with remorse extinguish now my sorrow!
Renew those lamps which thy disdain hath quenched,
As Phœbus doth his sister Phœbe's shine;
Consider how thy Corin being drenched
In seas of woe, to thee his plaints incline,
And at thy feet with tears doth sue for grace,
Which art the goddess of his chaste desire;
Let not thy frowns these labours poor deface
Although aloft they at the first aspire;
    And time shall come as yet unknown to men
    When I more large thy praises forth shall pen!

XLIV

When I more large thy praises forth shall show,
That all the world thy beauty shall admire,
Desiring that most sacred nymph to know
Which hath the shepherd's fancy set on fire;
Till then, my dear, let these thine eyes content,
Till then, fair love, think if I merit favour,
Till then, O let thy merciful assent
Relish my hopes with some comforting savour;
So shall you add such courage to my muse
That she shall climb the steep Parnassus hill,
That learnèd poets shall my deeds peruse
When I from thence obtainèd have more skill;
   And what I sing shall always be of thee
   As long as life or breath remains in me!

XLV

When she was born whom I entirely love,
Th' immortal gods her birth-rites forth to grace,
Descending from their glorious seat above,
They did on her these several virtues place:
First Saturn gave to her sobriety,
Jove then induèd her with comeliness,
And Sol with wisdom did her beautify,
Mercury with wit and knowledge did her bless,
Venus with beauty did all parts bedeck,
Luna therewith did modesty combine,
Diana chaste all loose desires did check,
And like a lamp in clearness she doth shine.
    But Mars, according to his stubborn kind,
    No virtue gave, but a disdainful mind.

XLVI

When Chloris first with her heart-robbing eye
Inchanted had my silly senses all,
I little did respect love's cruelty,
I never thought his snares should me enthrall;
But since her tresses have entangled me,
My pining flock did never hear me sing
Those jolly notes which erst did make them glee,
Nor do my kids about me leap and spring
As they were wont, but when they hear me cry
They likewise cry and fill the air with bleating;
Then do my sheep upon the cold earth lie,
And feed no more, my griefs they are repeating.
    O Chloris, if thou then saw'st them and me
    I'm sure thou wouldst both pity them and me!

XLVII

I need not tell thee of the lily white,
Nor of the roseate red which doth thee grace,
Nor of thy golden hairs like Phœbus bright,
Nor of the beauty of thy fairest face.
Nor of thine eyes which heavenly stars excel,
Nor of thine azured veins which are so clear,
Nor of thy paps where Love himself doth dwell,
Which like two hills of violets appear.
Nor of thy tender sides, nor belly soft,
Nor of thy goodly thighs as white as snow,
Whose glory to my fancy seemeth oft
That like an arch triumphal they do show.
    All these I know that thou dost know too well,
    But of thy heart too cruel I thee tell.

XLVIII

But of thy heart too cruel I thee tell,
Which hath tormented my young budding age,
And doth, unless your mildness passions quell,
My utter ruin near at hand presage.
Instead of blood which wont was to display
His ruddy red upon my hairless face,
By over-grieving that is fled away,
Pale dying colour there hath taken place.
Those curlèd locks which thou wast wont to twist
Unkempt, unshorn, and out of order been;
Since my disgrace I had of them no list,
Since when these eyes no joyful day have seen
    Nor never shall till you renew again
    The mutual love which did possess us twain.

XLIX

You that embrace enchanting poesy,
Be gracious to perplexèd Corin's lines;
You that do feel love's proud authority,
Help me to sing my sighs and sad designs.
Chloris, requite not faithful love with scorn,
But as thou oughtest have commiseration;
I have enough anatomised and torn
My heart, thereof to make a pure oblation.
Likewise consider how thy Corin prizeth
Thy parts above each absolute perfection,
How he of every precious thing deviseth
To make thee sovereign. Grant me then affection!
    Else thus I prize thee: Chloris is alone
    More hard than gold or pearl or precious stone.

INTRODUCTION

By Martha Foote Crow

The last decade of the sixteenth century was marked by an outburst of
sonneteering. To devotees of the sonnet, who find in that poetic form the
most perfect vehicle that has ever been devised for the expression of a
single importunate emotion, it will not seem strange that at the threshold
of a literary period whose characteristic note is the most intense
personality, the instinct of poets should have directed them to the form
most perfectly fitted for the expression of this inner motive.

The sonnet, a distinguished guest from Italy, was ushered to by
those two "courtly makers," Sir Thomas Wyatt and the Earl of Surrey
(Henry Howard), in the days of Henry VIII. But when, forty years
later, the foreigner was to be acclimatised in England, her robe had to
be altered to suit an English fashion. Thus the sonnet, which had been
an octave of enclosed or alternate rhymes, followed by a sestette of
interlaced tercets, was now changed to a series of three quatrains with
differing sets of alternate rhymes in each, at the close of which the
insidious couplet succeeded in establishing itself. But these changes
were not made without a great deal of experiment; and during the
tentative period the name "sonnet" was given to a wide variety of forms,
in the moulding of which but one rule seemed to be uniformly obeyed –
that the poem should be the expression of a single, simple emotion. This
law cut the poem to a relative shortness and defined its dignity and
clearness. Beyond this almost every combination of rhymes might be
found, verses were occasionally lengthened or shortened, and the
number of lines in the poem, though generally fourteen, showed

considerable variation.

The sonnet-sequence was also a suggestion from Italy, a literary fashion introduced by Sir Philip Sidney, in his *Astrophel and Stella*, written soon after 1580, but not published till 1591. In a sonnet-cycle Sidney recorded his love and sorrow, and Edmund Spenser took up the strain with his story of love and joy. Grouped about these, and following in their wake, a number of poets, before the decade was over, turned this Elizabethan "toy" to their purpose in their various self-revealings, producing a group of sonnet-cycles more or less purpose in their various self-revealings, producing a group of sonnet-cycles more or less Italianate in form or thought, more or less experimental, more or less poetical, more or less the expression of a real passion. For while the form of the sonnet was modified by metrical traditions and habits, the content also was strongly influenced, not to say restricted, by certain conventions of thought considered at the time appropriate to the poetic attitude. The passion for classic colour in the poetic world, which had inspired and disciplined English genius in the sixties and seventies, was rather nourished than repressed when in the eighties Spenser's *Shepherd's Calendar* and Sidney's *Arcadia* made the pastoral imagery a necessity. Cupid and Diana were made very much at home in the golden world of the Renaissance Arcadia, and the sonneteer singing the praises of his mistress's eyebrow was not far removed from the lovelorn shepherd of the plains.

It may reasonably be expected that in any sonnet-cycle there will be found many sonnets in praise of the loved one's beauty, many lamenting her hardness of heart; all the wonders of heaven and earth will be catalogued to find comparisons for her loveliness; the river by which she dwells will be more pleasant than all other rivers in the world, a list of them being appended in proof; the thoughts of night-time, when the lover bemoans himself and his rejected state, or dreams of happy love, will be dwelt upon; oblivious sleep and the wan-faced moon will be invoked, and death will be called upon for respite. Love and the praises of the loved one was the theme. On this old but ever new refrain the sonneteer devised his descant, trilling joyously on oaten pipe in praise of Delia or Phyllis, Cœlia, Cælica, Aurora, or Castara.

But this melody and descant were not, in some ears at least, without monotony. For after Samuel Daniel's *Delia*, Henry Constable's *Diana*, Thomas Lodge's *Phillis*, Michael Drayton's *Idea*, Giles Fletcher's *Licia*,

Brooke's *Cœlica*, William Percy's *Cœlia*, N.L.'s *Zepheria*, and J.C.'s *Alcilia*, and perhaps a few other sonnet-cycles had been written, George Chapman in 1595 made his *Coronet for his Mistress Philosophy*, the opening sonnet of which reveals his critical attitude:

> "Muses that sing Love's sensual empery,
> And lovers kindling your enragèd fires
> At Cupid's bonfires burning in the eye,
> Blown with the empty breath of vain desires,
> You that prefer the painted cabinet
> Before the wealthy jewels it doth store ye,
> That all your joys in dying figures set,
> And stain the living substance of your glory,
> Abjure those joys, abhor their memory,
> And let my love the honoured subject be
> Of love, and honour's complete history;
> Your eyes were never yet let in to see
> The majesty and riches of the mind,
> But dwell in darkness; for your god is blind."

It must be confessed that the "painted cabinet" of the lady's beauty absorbs more attention than the "majesty and riches of the mind," but the glints of a loftier ideal shining now and then among the conventions, lift the cycle above the level of mere ear-pleasing rhythms and fantastical imageries. Moreover, the sonnet-cycles on the whole show an independence and spontaneousness of poetic energy, a delight in the pure joy of making, a *naïveté*, that richly frame the picture of the golden world they present. When Thomas Lodge, addressing his "pleasing thoughts, apprentices of love," cries out:

> "Show to the world, though poor and scant my skill is,
> How sweet thoughts be that are but thought on Phillis,"

we feel that we are being taken back to an age more childlike than our own; and when the sonneteers vie with each other on the themes of sleep, death, time, and immortality, the door often stands open toward sublimity. Then when the sonnet-cycle was consecrated to noble and spiritual uses in George Chapman's *Coronet for his Mistress Philosophy*, Barnabe Barnes's *Divine Century of Spiritual Sonnets*, Genry Constable's *Spiritual Sonnets in Honour of God and His Saints*, and John Donne's *Holy Sonnets*, all made before 1600, the symbolic theme was added to the conventions of the sonnet-realm, the scope of its content was broadened; and the sonnet was well on its way toward a time when it could be named a trumpet, upon which a mighty voice could blow soul-animating strains.

One of the most fascinating questions in the study of the sonnet-cycles is as to how much basis the story has in reality. Stella we know, the star-crossed love of Sir Philip Sidney, and Edmund Spenser's happy Elizabeth, but –

"Who is Silvia? What is she
That all the swains commend her?"

Who is Delia, Diana, Cœlia, Cælica, and all the rhyming of musical names? And who is the Dark Lady? What personalities hide behind these poet's imaginings? We know that now, as in troubadour days, the praises of grand ladies were sung with a warmth of language that should indicate personal acquaintance when no such acquaintance existed; and the sonneteers sometimes frankly confessed their passion "but supposed." All this adds to the difficulty of interpretation. In most cases the poet has effectually kept his secret; the search is futile, in spite of all the "scholastic labour-lost" devoted to it. Equally tantalising are the fleeting symbolisms that suggest themselves now and then. The confession sometimes made by the poet, that high-flown compliment and not true despair is intended, prepares us to accept the symbolic application where it forces itself upon us, and to feel the presence here and there of platonic or spiritual shadowings. Those who do not find pleasure in the Arcadian world of the sonneteer's fancy, may still justify their taste in the aspiration that speaks in his flashes of philosophy.

THOMAS LODGE: *PHILLIS*

By Martha Foote Crow

One of the first to take up the new fashion of the sonnet-cycle, was Thomas Lodge, whose *Phillis* was published in 1595. Lodge had a wide acquaintance among the authors of his time, and was in the thick of the literary activity in the last two decades of the sixteenth century. But in spite of his interesting personality and genius, he has had to wait until the present time for full appreciation. To his own age he may have appeared as a literary dilettante, who tried his hand at several forms of writing, and being outshone by the more excellent in each field, gave up the attempt and turned to the practice of medicine. This profession engaged him for the last twenty-five years of his life, until his death in 1625 at the advanced age of sixty-seven or eight. During all these years the gay young "university wit" of earlier days was probably forgotten in the venerable and successful physician. It was as "old Doctor Lodge" that he was satirised in a Cambridge student's Common-place Book in 1611. Heywood mentions him in 1609 among the six most famous physicians in England, and in the *Return from Parnassus*, a play acted in 1602, he is described as "turning over Galen every day."

Yet no one had been in the last twenty years the sixteenth century more responsive than Thomas Lodge to the shifting moods of that excitable period. Lodge was the son of a Lord Mayor of London, and was a contemporary at Oxford with Sidney, Gosson, Chapman, Lyly, Peele and Watson. His life included a round of varied experiences. A student at Lincoln's Inn, a young aspirant for literary honours, friends with Robert Greene, Rich, Samuel Daniel, Michael Drayton, John Lyly and Thomas Watson, a taster of the sorrows that many of the University wits endured when usurers got their hands upon them, for a time perhaps a soldier, certainly a sailor following the fortunes of Captain Clarke to Terceras and the Canaries, and of Cavendish to Brazil and the Straits of Magellan, in London again making plays with Greene, off to Avignon to take his degree in medicine, back again to be incorporated an M.D. at Oxford and to practise in London, adopting secretly the Roman Catholic faith, and sometimes hiding on the continent as a recusant from persecution at home, imprisoned perhaps once for debt, and entertaining a concourse of patients of his own religion till his death in 1625: – the life of Lodge thus presents a view of the ups and downs possible in that picturesque age.

The wide variety of his literary ventures reflects the interests of his life. Some controversial papers, some unsuccessful plays, two dull historical sketches in prose, some satirical and moralising works in prose and in verse, two romantic tales in verse and three in prose, a number of eclogues, metrical epistles and lyrics, some ponderous translations from Latin and French, and two medical treatises; these widely differing kinds of writing are the products of Thomas Lodge's industry and genius. All, however, have but an antiquarian interest save two; the prose romance called *Rosalynde, Euphues' Golden Legacy*, could not be spared since William Shakespeare borrowed its charming plot for *As You Like It*; and *Phillis*, bound up with a sheaf of his lyrics gathered from the pages of his stories and from the miscellanies of the time, should be treasured for its own sake and should keep Lodge's memory green for lovers of pure poetry.

Thomas Lodge's lyric genius was a clear if slender rill. His faults are the more unpardonable since they spring from sheer carelessness and a lack of appreciation of the sacred responsibility of creative power. He took up the literary fashion of the month and tried his hand at it; that done, he was ready for the next mode. He did not wait to perfect his work or to compare result with result; therefore he probably never found himself, probably never realised that after three centuries he would be esteemed, not for the ponderous tomes of his translation of Josephus, not for all the catalogues of his satirical and religious and scientific writings, but for mere lyrics like the "Heigh ho, fair Rosaline," and "Love in my bosom like a bee," heedlessly imbedded in the heart of a prose romance.

Thomas Lodge was one of the earliest to follow the example of Sir Philip Sidney in linking a sequence of sonnets together into a sonnet-cycle. The *Astrophel and Stella* was published in 1591, though it had doubtless before this been handed about, as was the Elizabethan fashion, in manuscript. Early in 1591 also when Samuel Daniel was probably abroad, twenty-seven of the fifty-seven sonnets that a year later formed the sonnet-cycle *Delia* were published in his absence. Now in August of 1591 Thomas Lodge set sail with Cavendish on that long voyage to Brazil and the Straits of Magellan from which he did not return till early in ninety-three, and it was during his absence that Daniel's and Henry Constable's sonnet-cycles came out. It is possible that Lodge saw Daniel's series, as he doubtless did Sidney's, in manuscript before he left England, but the Induction to *Phillis*, which carries a message to Delia's "sweet prophet," was almost certainly written later, and in the absence of further proof it seems no more than fair to allow Lodge to share with Daniel and Constable the honour of being the earliest to take the hint Sidney had offered.

On the whole, Thomas Lodge's sonnets show a much more cheerful and buoyant temper than Samuel Daniel's "wailing verse." The "sad horror, pale grief, prostrate despair" that inform the Daniel's "wailing verse." The "sad horror, pale grief, prostrate despair" that inform the *Delia*, are replaced in the *Phillis* by a spirit of airy toying, a pleasure in the graces of fancy even when they cluster around a feeling of sadness. During Lodge's absence, his friend Robert Greene published several pieces for him, and in one of the prefaces promised the public to present on his return "what labours Lodge's sea-studies afford." *Phillis* was the chief of these sea-studies, and was like *Rosalynde* "hatcht in the stormes of the ocean and feathered in the surges of many perillous seas." But as far as the imagery of the sonnets is concerned, the pageantry of day and night at sea might have passed before blinded eyes; if it made any impression, it was in the form of ocean-nymphs and Cupid at the helm. The poet was in Arcadia, Phillis was a shepherdess, and the conventional imageries of the pastoral valley were the environment. "May it please you," he says in dedicating the book to the Countess of Shrewsbury, "to looke and like of homlie Phillis in her Country caroling, and to countenance her poore and affectionate sheapheard." The Countess of Shrewsbury he chooses for the "Sovereign and she-Mæcenas" of his toil, and promises her "as much in affection as any other can performe in perfection;" but the name of Phillis is no cover for the personality of a grand lady, and therefore no puzzling questions disturb the pleasure of the reader as the gentle modulations, the insidious alliterations, and the musical cadences of his double rhymes fall upon the ear.

Yet for this name or ideal, or whatever Phillis represented in the poet's thought, he has poured forth a passion that has an air of sincerity, an artless freshness, a flute-like clearness of tone, as rare as delightful. It is the very voice of the oaten pipe itself, thin, clear, and pure. The touches of seriousness are impossible, to mistake. When the poet avows his faith in Phillis' constancy, after giving the usual catalogue of her beauties, he says:

> "At thy fair hands who wonders not at all
> Wonder itself through ignorance embases;
> Yet not the less though wondrous gifts you call these
> My faith is far more wonderful than all these."

When Phillis persists in her disdain, he cries out impulsively:

> "Burst, burst, poor heart, thou hast no longer hope!"

Even when re-moulding the familiar pastoral conceits, he makes the fancies his own and gives to them a unique touch and spirit. Mere conventions he rates at their proper value. His pen shall not "riot in pompous style." He claims a brighter aspect for his poetical devotion than his fellow-sonneteers manifest:

> "No stars her; eyes....
> ... but beams that clear the sight
> Of him that seeks the true philosophy."

In spite of its defects, the lax structure of the sonnet-form, the obscurities and needless blurring, and the disappointing inequalities, *Phillis* takes a high place among the sonnet-cycles, and must ever be dear to lovers of quiet, melodious verse, who have made themselves at home in the golden world of the pastoral poets and mislike not the country-carolling heard therein.

GILES FLETCHER: *LICIA*

By Martha Foote Crow

Giles Fletcher, author of *Licia*, was one of that distinguished family that included Richard Fletcher, the Bishop of London, and his son John Fletcher, the dramatist. The two sons of Dr. Giles Fletcher were also men of marked poetic ability: Phineas, the author of that extraordinary allegorical poem, *The Purple Island*; and Giles, of *Christ's Victory and Triumph*. There was a strong family feeling in this circle; Phineas and Giles pay compliments to each other in their verse and show great reverence and tenderness toward the memory of the poetic powers of their father. But Giles Fletcher the elder was not thought of in his own time as a poet. Educated at Eton and Trinity, Cambridge, where he was made LL.D. in 1581, a member of Parliament in '85, employed in many public services at home and abroad during a career that lasted until 1611, in which year Dr. Fletcher died at the age of seventy-two, he was known as a man of action, a man for public responsibility, rather than as the retired scholar or riming courtier. Most important among the foreign embassages undertaken by Fletcher was the one to Russia. The results were of great import to England, commercially and otherwise, but the book he wrote on his return was, for political reasons, suppressed.

It happened that the years of enforced idleness that followed the suppression of this book came in the time when the young sonneteers at London were all busy. He returned from his embassage in '89; the book was suppressed in '91. *Licia* was published in '93. The writing of *Licia* was "rather an effect than a cause of idleness;" he did it "only to try his humor," he says apologetically in the dedicatory addresses.

> Whereas my thoughts and some reasons drew me rather to have dealt in causes of greater weight, yet the present jar of this disagreeing age drives me into a fit so melancholy, as I had only leisure to grow passionate.

In case wise heads should think him to be treating "an idle subject and so frivolous," or that it has been "vainly handled and so odious," he sets forth the nobility of his view.

> Howsoever, Love in this age hath behaved himself in that loose manner as it is counted a disgrace to give him but a kind look, yet I take the passion in itself to be of that honor and credit, as it is a perfect resemblance of the greatest happiness, and rightly valued at his just price (in a mind that is sincerely and truly amorous), an affection of greatest virtue and able of himself to eternise the meanest vassal.

"For Love," he declares,

> is a goddess (pardon me though I speak like a poet) not respecting the contentment of him that loves, but the virtues of the beloved; satisfied with wondering, fed with admiration; respecting nothing but his lady's worthiness; made as happy by love as by all favors; chaste by honor; far from violence; respecting but one, and that one in such kindness, honesty, truth, constancy, and honor, as were all the world offered to make a change, yet the boot were too small and therefore bootless. This is love, and far more than this, which I know a vulgar head, a base mind, an ordinary conceit, a common person will not nor cannot have. Thus do I commend that love wherewith in these poems I have honoured the worthy Licia.

The sonnet-cycle is inscribed "To the worthie kinde wise and virtuous ladie, the Ladie Mollineux; wife to the right worshipful Sir Richard Mollineux Knight." Nothing is known of this lady, except that her family may possibly have been very distantly connected with that of Giles Fletcher. What the poet's feeling was towards his patroness he defines sufficiently.

> Now in that I have written love sonnets, if any man measure my affection by my style, let him say I am in love... Yet take this by the way; though I am so liberal to grant thus much, a man may write of love and not be in love, as well as of husbandry and not go to the plough, or of witches and be none, or of holiness and be flat profane.

What "shadowings" the poet may intend he refuses to confide to us.

> If thou muse what my Licia is, take her to be some Diana, at the least
> chaste; or some Minerva; no Venus, fairer far. It may be she is Learning's
> image, or some heavenly wonder, which the preciesest may not dislike:
> perhaps under that name I have shadowed Discipline. It may be I mean that
> kind courtesy which I found at the patroness of these poems. It may be some
> college; it may be my conceit, and portend nothing.

It is evident then that the patroness herself is not the real person
behind the poetic title. He therefore dedicates *Licia* to Lady Molineux,
not because the sonnets themselves are addressed to her, but because he
has received "favours undeserved" at her hands and those of "wise Sir
Richard" for which he "wants means to make recompence," and
therefore in the meantime he begs her to accept this. "If thou like it," he
says to the reader,

> take it, and thank the worthy Lady Mollineux, for whose sake thou hast it;
> worthy, indeed, and so not only reputed by me in private affection of
> thankfulness but so equally to be esteemed by all that know her. For if I had
> not received of her... those unrequitable favours, I had not thus idly toyed.

A warm admirer of Giles Fletcher has expressed his opinion that
Licia "sparkles with brilliants of the first water." A more temperate
judgment is that of another, who says that he "took part without
discredit in the choir of singers who were men of action too." *Licia* is
what a typical sonnet-cycle ought to be, a delicate and almost
intangible thread of story on which are strung the separate sonnet-
pearls. In this case the jewels have a particular finish. Fletcher has
adopted the idea of a series of quatrains, often extending the number to
four, and a concluding couplet, which he seems fond of utilising to give
an epigrammatic finish to the ingenious incident he so often makes the
subject of the sonnet. He is fully in the spirit of the Italian mode,
however, acknowledging in his title page his indebtedness to poets of
other nationalities than his own.

BARTHOLOMEW GRIFFIN: *FIDESSA*

By Martha Foote Crow

The author of *Fidessa* has gained undeserved notice from the fact that the piratical printer W. Jaggard, included a transcript of one of his sonnets in a volume that he put forth in 1599, under the name of William Shakespeare. It would be easy to believe, in spite of the doubtful rimes characteristic of *Fidessa*, that sonnet three was not Bartholomew Griffin's, for no singer in the Elizabethan choir was more skilful in turning his voice to other people's melodies than was he. He has been called "a gross plagiary;" yet it must be realised that the sonneteers of that time felt they had a right, almost a duty, to take up the poetic themes used by their models. Griffin shows great ingenuity in the manipulation of the stock-themes, and the lover of Francesco Petrarch and all the young Abraham-Slenders of the day must have been delighted with the familiar "designs" as they re-appeared in *Fidessa*.

Bartholomew Griffin was buried in Coventry in 1602. In 1596 he dedicated his "slender work" *Fidessa* to William Essex of Lamebourne in Berkshire. He adds an address to the Gentlemen of the Inns of Court, whom he begs to "censure mildly as protectors of a poor stranger" and "judge the best as encouragers of a young beginner." Of the poet little further is known. From the sonnets themselves we learn that Fidessa was "of high regard," the child of a beautiful mother and of a renowned father; she sprang in fact from the same root with the poet himself, who writes "Gent." after his name on the title-page. She had been kind to him in sickness and had "yielded to each look of his a sweet reply." After giving these slight hints, he pushes forth from the moorings of realism and sets sail on the ocean of the sonneteer's fancy, meeting the usual adventures. His sonnets, while showing versatility and ingenuity, lack spontaneous feeling and have serious defects in form; yet these defects are in part offset by their conversational ease and dramatic vividness.

WILLIAM SMITH: *CHLORIS*

By Martha Foote Crow

The sub-title of *Chloris* arouses an expectation that is gratified in the pastoral modishness of the sonnets. Corin sits under the "lofty pines, co-partners of his woe," with oaten reed at his lips, and calls on sylvans, lambkins and all Parnassans to testify to the beauty and cruelty of Chloris. The attitude is a self-conscious one, yet the poem reveals little of the personality of the author beyond the facts of his youthfulness and of his devotion to "the most excellent and learned Shepheard, Colin Cloute." It was in 1595, but one year before the publication of *Chloris*, that Edmund Spenser had sung his own sonnets of true love, and it is perhaps on this account that William Smith finds him in a mood favourable to the defence of a young aspirant. At any rate, the language of the dedication rings with something more than mere desire for distinguished patronage. The youth looks with a beautiful humility upward toward the greater but "dear and most entire beloved" poet. His own sonnets, he says, are "of my study the budding springs"; they are but "young-hatched orphan things." He nowhere boasts that they will give immortal renown to the scornful beauty, but modestly promises that if her cruel disdain does not ruin him, the time shall come when he "more large" her "praises forth shall pen." *Chloris* had once been favourable, as sonnet forty-eight distinctly shows, but the cycle does not bring any happy conclusion to the story. Corin is left weeping but faithful, and the picture of *Chloris* is composed of such faint outlines only as the sonneteer's conventions can delineate. Beyond this no certain information in regard to poet or honoured lady has yet been unearthed.

For all its formality, however, the sonnet-cycle is not wanting in touches of real feeling and lines of musical sweetness; the writer shows considerable skill in the management of rime, and in structure he adopts the form preferred by William Shakespeare, whose "sugared sonnets" may by this date have passed beneath his eye. The melodies piped by other sonnet-shepherds re-echo with a great deal of distinctness in Covin's strains; nevertheless he has himself taken a draught from the true Elizabethan fount of lyric inspiration, and the nymph Chloris with her heart-robbing eye well deserves a place on the snow-soft downs where the sonneteering shepherds were wont to assemble.

HENRY CONSTABLE: *DIANA*

By Mark Tuley

Henry Constable was born in 1562; he studied at Cambridge (1580); converted to Catholicism around 1590; he worked as a spy in Europe, returning to England in 1603. He died in Liège in 1613 after being arrested in 1604 (after which he lived in poverty), and banished in 1610.

Henry Constable's *Diana: The Praises of His Mistress In Certain Sweete Sonnets* was published first in 1592 (it contained only 23 sonnets). There is some confusion about which of the *Diana* sonnets Constable wrote (Constable was in Europe at the time), in the 1594 edition (*Diana or the Excellent Conceitful Sonnets of H.C. Augmented With Divers Quatorzains of Honorable and Lerned Personages*). In the later, 1594 *Diana*, there are 8 decades of 76 sonnets. Some of the sonnets were written by Sir Philip Sidney (as indicated).

The identity of Diana is unknown, although Henry Constable did address some sonnets to Lady Rich, the woman who inspired Stella in Sir Philip Sidney's *Astrophel and Stella*.

FURTHER READING

HIGHLY RECOMMENDED

The following books are excellent introductions to the Elizabethan sonnet. Maurice Evans' *Elizabethan Sonnets* (1977, later revised, in 1994) is one of the best books as an all-round collection of Elizabethan sonneteering.

Maurice Evans, ed. *Elizabethan Sonnets*, Dent, 1977/ 94
G. Hiller, ed. *Poems of the Elizabethan Age*, Methuen, 1977
E. Lucie-Smith, ed. *The Penguin Book of Elizabethan Verse*, Penguin, 1965
Michael R.G. Spiller. *The Development of the Sonnet: An Introduction*, Routledge, 1992
Maurice Valency. *In Praise of Love: An Introduction to the Love-Poetry of the Renaissance*, Macmillan, New York, 1961

OTHER BOOKS

Books marked with an asterisk are especially useful.

Sandra Berman. *The Sonnet Over Time*, Chapel Hill, 1988*
Harold Bloom, ed. *Shakespeare's Sonnets*, Chelsea House, New York, 1987
—. *Hamlet*, Chelsea House, New York, 1990
S. Booth. *An Essay on Shakespeare's Sonnets*, Yale University Press, 1969
S.C. Campbell. *Only Begotten Sonnets: A Reconstruction of Shakespeare's Sonnets Sequence*, Bell & Hyman, 1978
Reed Way Dasenbrock. *Imitating the Italians: Wyatt, Spenser, Synge, Pound, Joyce*, John Hopkins University Press, Baltimore, 1991
Heather Dubrow. *Captive Victors: Shakespeare's Narrative Poems and Sonnets*, Cornell University Press, Ithaca, 1987
—. *Echoes of Desire: English Petrarchism and Its Counter-discourses*, Cornell University Press, 1995 *
Joel Fineman. *Shakespeare's Perjured Eye: The Invention of Poetic Subjectivity in the Sonnets*, University of California Press, 1988*
Edward Hubler. *The Sense of Shakespeare's Sonnets*, Hill & Wang, New York,

J.B. Leishman. *Themes and Variations in Shakespeare's Sonnets*, Hillary House, New York, 1963

J. W. Lever. *The Elizabethan Love Sonnet*, Methuen, 1956

Arthur Marotti. ""Love is not love": Elizabethan Sonnet Sequences and the Social Order", *English Literary History*, 49, 1982

Kenneth Muir. *Shakespeare's Sonnets*, Allen & Unwin, 1979

G.M. Ridden. *Shakespeare's Sonnets*, Longman, 1982

Brent Stirling. *The Shakespeare Sonnet Order: Poems and Groups*, University of California Press, Berkeley, 1968

J.C. Wait. *The Background to Shakespeare's Sonnets*, Chatto & Windus, 1972

James Winny. *The Master-Mistress: A Study of Shakespeare's Sonnets*, Chatto & Windus, 1968